A BARD OF WOLFE'S ARMY:

JAMES THOMPSON, GENTLEMAN VOLUNTEER, 17

Cover illustration. "The Pinch of Snuff" (c.1760) by French painter William Delacour depicts, according to the late John Telfer Dunbar, one of Scotland's leading dress experts, a 42nd officer or 77th officer "in the American campaign" taking a pinch of snuff and holding an ornate broadsword under his left arm. Dunbar forgot that a third Highland battalion also soldiered in the New World – the 78th Foot, more commonly known as Fraser's Highlanders. The officer's facings on cuffs and collars are off-white, most definitely the facings of the 78th.

The title helps us identify the sitter with some certainty. The regimental absent officers' list shows "Ens[ign] Malcolm MacPherson gone to England 18th Octb^r 1759 by General Monckton's leave." The oldest officer in Fraser's Highlanders and an expert swordsman, Malcom Macpherson of Phoness, a fellow gentleman volunteer until his promotion just before the battle on the Plains of Abraham, would have been well known to our hero James Thompson, a fellow snuff-taker. Part of Brigadier General George Townshend's retinue of officers that accompanied him back to England, Macpherson was presented to King George II. The king graciously extended his hand to the brave Highlander for the usual salute, but being unversed in court etiquette, the old Highlander placed his snuff-box in the king's hand and "shook the royal palm with both hands with such ardour and emotion that the king was fain to cry out for quarter. Realising that anything but disrespect was meant, the King at once partook of a pinch from MacPherson's Badenoch mull."

This "Pinch of Snuff" incident was widely reported back in Scotland during the winter of 1759–60. In London Macpherson became something of a celebrity, being frequently pointed out with the remark, "There goes the brave old Highlander with his famous sword." He returned to a hero's welcome in Scotland in early 1760, where he was made a free burgess and guild brother of the City of Edinburgh for his good services, "but particularly for the bravery for which he behaved at the Battle of Quebec." Interestingly, some Jacobite Freemasons were known as "Snuff-takers" and took the tobacco leaf as their emblem. Many snuff mulls such as the one held in this painting contained hidden portraits of Bonnie Prince Charlie or were carved with secret Jacobean symbols. One can only speculate that "Old Phoness" may actually have pressed a Jacobite mull into King George's hand and that this 1760 portrait might be a tribute to the old Jacobite's "in-your-face" audacity and sangfroid. (Private Collection)

"The Gallant Old Highlander." A pen and ink sketch of James Thompson in his ninety-fifth year by Captain John Crawford Young of the 79th Highlanders made on 9 September 1828 and presumably taken back to Scotland by the Earl of Dalhousie, Young's patron and mentor. It would appear that a second sketch was left with James Thompson and, in later years, when photography was invented, copies were made and distributed to various family members. One of these photographic copies was acquired by Masonic historian Alfred J. B. Milborne (1888–1976). The location of the two original sketches is unknown. (LAC R3052-0-6-E.)

A BARD OF WOLFE'S ARMY

James Thompson, Gentleman Volunteer, 1733–1830

Edited by Earl John Chapman & Ian Macpherson McCulloch

Foreword by Dr. D. Peter MacLeod
Historian, Pre-Confederation, Canadian War Museum

Published in collaboration with the Stewart Museum
(The Fort, Île-Ste-Hélène, Montreal) and the 78th Fraser Highlanders

ROBIN BRASS STUDIO
Montreal

Copyright © Earl John Chapman and Ian Macpherson McCulloch 2010

All rights reserved. No part of this publication may be stored in a retrieval system, transmitted or reproduced in any form or by any means, photocopying, electronic or mechanical, without written permission of the publisher or a licence from the Canadian Copyright Licensing Agency (Access Copyright). For an Access Copyright licence, visit <www.accesscopyright.ca> or call 1-800-893-5777.

Published 2010 by Robin Brass Studio Inc.
www.rbstudiobooks.com

Paperback: ISBN-13: 978-1-896941-62-2 (ISBN-10: 1-896941-62-1)
Hardcover: ISBN-13: 978-1-896941-63-9 (ISBN-10: 1-896941-63-X)

Printed and bound in Canada by Marquis Imprimeur Inc., Cap-Saint-Ignace, Quebec

Library and Archives Canada Cataloguing in Publication

Thompson, James, 1732–1830
   A bard of Wolfe's army : James Thompson, gentleman volunteer, 1733–1830 / edited by Earl John Chapman & Ian Macpherson McCulloch.

"Published in collaboration with the Stewart Museum (The Fort, Île-Ste-Hélène, Montreal) and the 78th Fraser Highlanders".

Includes bibliographical references and index.
ISBN 978-1-896941-62-2 (pbk.). – ISBN 978-1-896941-63-9 (bound)

   1. Thompson, James, 1732–1830. 2. Wolfe, James, 1727–1759. 3. Canada – History – Seven Years' War, 1755–1763 – Campaigns. 4. Québec (Province) – History – 18th century. 5. Soldiers – Scotland – Biography. I. Chapman, Earl John. II. McCulloch, Ian M., 1954– . III. David M. Stewart Museum. IV. 78th Fraser Highlanders. V. Title.

FC384.T56 2010   971.01'88   C2010-904696-X

To James Thompson Junior, the proud son and the first true editor of *A Bard of Wolfe's Army*. He had the wit to recognize the historical value of his father's eyewitness accounts and took it upon himself to diligently and patiently transcribe each and every oral history. For his foresighted actions in preserving his father's deeds and exploits for posterity, we are forever in his debt.

"A loyal and dutiful son." A photograph of James Thompson Junior in his eighty-fourth year, resplendent in the full dress uniform of a deputy commissary general. Photographed in Quebec City in 1867, James was permitted to wear his uniform on special occasions, although he had been retired and placed on the half-pay list in 1846. (LAC C-052167.)

CONTENTS

Foreword by Dr. D. Peter MacLeod, Historian, Pre-Confederation,
   Canadian War Museum   xi
Acknowledgments   xiii
Abbreviations and Note on Typography   xiv
Introduction   xv

PART ONE

A "BROTHER SOLDIER..."
JAMES THOMPSON AND THE WOLFE LEGACY   3
   A Colour Album   102

PART TWO

"WHACK WENT THE BROADSWORD!"
THE REMINISCENCES OF SERGEANT JAMES THOMPSON   111
   1. Raised for Overseas Service, 1757   111
   2. Winter Quarters, Connecticut Colony, 1757–58   125
   3. The Siege and Capture of Louisbourg, 1758   133
   4. Winter Quarters, New York Colony, 1758–59   164
   5. The Siege and Battle for Quebec, 1759   171
   6. Winter Garrison and the Battle of Sillery, 1759–60   190
   7. The Reduction of Montreal, 1760   210
   8. Garrisoning the St. Lawrence, 1760–63   220
   9. The American Revolution and Siege of Quebec, 1775–76   230
  10. Miscellanea   240

PART THREE

BIOGRAPHICAL NOTES   253

APPENDICES

Appendix A: Anecdote 38 – Memorandum of the Most Arduous Services
   Performed by James Thompson ...   329
Appendix B: List of Anecdotes   337

Bibliography   340
Index   348

MAPS

"A Plan of the City of Quebec…," Jeffreys, 1760	2
"Plan of the Town of Quebec…," Mackellar, 1759	14–15
The Quebec Area, 1759	17
James Thompson's Quebec, 1830, Bouchette	98–99
Canadian Theatre of Operations, 1759	110
"Map of the Province of Nova Scotia and Parts adjacent…," Turner, 1759	134
The Long Haul… General Robert Monckton's Camp at Pointe Lévy	187
Sillery: The Culminating Point	198
Montreal in 1761, Labrosse	216
Assault on Quebec: Approach Routes of Generals Montgomery and Arnold	232

FOREWORD

Every day, in schools, museums, universities and homes across Canada, veterans talk about their service in war and peace from the Second World War to Afghanistan. Their stories bridge the gap between people for whom these conflicts are comfortably distant in time and space and those for whom they are lived experience.

James Thompson fulfilled a similar role for the Seven Years' War and American Revolution in Canada. A veteran of the siege of Louisbourg in 1758 and three sieges of Quebec – by the British in 1759, the French in 1760 and American rebels in 1775–76 – Thompson lived out his postwar life in Quebec City. Surrounded by compatriots who wanted to hear more about these events, Thompson was more than pleased to oblige.

A born raconteur, Thompson spoke in close-ups rather than panoramas. Addressing informed listeners who were already familiar with Canada's recent military history, the former sergeant of the 78th Regiment of Foot (Fraser's Highlanders) gave them the human stories that only a veteran could provide.

In the course of his short but adventurous military career, Thompson met James Wolfe, who addressed him as "Brother Soldier," at the siege of Louisbourg, carried a wounded French soldier to an aid station after the Battle of the Plains of Abraham, and kept the sword of the commander of the American assault on Quebec City as a souvenir. Striking as they are, these are just three examples of a cascade of sparkling vignettes covering crime, scandal, valour, victory, defeat, honour, humour, a pet puppy and day-to-day life as a soldier.

Thompson's listeners found his stories engaging; to historians they are priceless. Speaking from no other motive than to entertain and amuse, Thompson provides a uniquely intimate glimpse of our military history from the perspective of a sergeant in the ranks. Any number of officers' accounts describe what happened at Louisbourg and Quebec; to find out what it was like to be there wearing a red coat, on the battlefield or back in camp, Thompson's anecdotes are the place to start.

When James Thompson died in 1830, British participation in the Seven Years' War in Canada passed out of living memory. Thompson himself might have been forgotten had not his son, another James, taken down the anecdotes in writing. Preserved for posterity in various archives and collections, these reminiscences were accessible only to scholars until two historians decided that Thompson deserved a wider audience. Earl Chapman and Ian McCulloch have performed a signal service to history by seeking out the surviving Thompson anecdotes and making them available to the public at large. In so doing, they have allowed Thompson to prolong his role as the "Bard of Wolfe's Army" into the twenty-first century.

D. Peter MacLeod
Historian, Pre-Confederation, Canadian War Museum

ACKNOWLEDGMENTS

The publication of a successful book is always the result of the efforts and co-operation of a great many people beyond those whose names appear on the title page. This is especially true in the case of *A Bard of Wolfe's Army.* The process involved everything from procuring a copy of the original journals to work from, to checking all the names, dates and places mentioned, so that our annotations properly interpret Thompson's story for the readers. Some people offered their technical expertise, others helped with digging through international archives, while some offered access to their extensive private collections.

Robin Brass at Robin Brass Studio Inc., as always, has done a superb job of designing and publishing the book. Another gentleman deserving special mention is the late William Forbes, a native of Perth, Scotland, a member of the Fort Stanwix 78th Pipe Band and a Highland scholar of great repute, who passed away before the publication of this book. Bill, graciously and patiently, helped us with numerous questions on James Thompson and his regiment right up to the day before he died in December 2009. He had also volunteered to be one of our final readers. Without the combined efforts of Robin, Bill and those listed below, this book would not have been possible, and we extend our sincerest thanks to all of you. If we have inadvertently missed anyone, we offer our deepest apologies.

Robert and Betty Andrews, Gananoque, Ontario; Bruce D. Bolton, David M. Stewart Museum, Montreal; Hugh Boscawen, London; Morag Ross Bremner, Tain and District Museum, Tain, Scotland; Dr. Steve Brumwell, Amsterdam; Joan Chapman, Roxboro, Quebec; René Chartrand, Aylmer, Quebec; James Dinan, Quebec City; Marie and Neil Fraser, Toronto; D. Paul Goodman, Île Perrot, Quebec; Louise Gunn, Quebec City; Dr. John Houlding, Ruckersdorf, Germany; Chris Johnson, Newcastle, Ontario; Pierre-Louis Lapointe, Bibliothèque et Archives nationales du Québec; Dr. D. Peter MacLeod, Canadian War Museum, Ottawa; Susan Johnson McCulloch, Toronto; David Miller, Military History and Diplomacy, Smithsonian Institution, Washington, D.C; Steve Noon; Prof. David R. O'Keefe, Montreal; Estelle Quick, Cromarty, Scotland; Lt. Col. Alain Quirion, Toronto; Glenn A. Steppler, London; John Torrance Stevenson, Toronto; Nicholas Westbrook, Crown Point, New York.

Abbreviations

The following abbreviations are used in the footnotes and picture credits.

BALs	British Army Lists
BAnQ	Bibliothèque et Archives nationales du Québec
CB	Commission Books, National Archives, Kew, U.K., WO 25
CHR	*Canadian Historical Review*
CO	Colonial Office Papers, National Archives, Kew, U.K.
CWM	Canadian War Museum, Ottawa
DAB	*Dictionary of American Biography*
DCB	*Dictionary of Canadian Biography*
DNB	*Dictionary of National Biography,* U.K.
HMS	His (or Her) Majesty's Ship
JSAHR	*Journal of the Society for Army Historical Research*
JGP	James Grant Papers, Library of Congress
JTC	James Thompson Collection, BAnQ
LAC	Library and Archives Canada, Ottawa
LOC	Library of Congress, Washington, D.C.
LHSQ	Literary and Historical Society of Quebec (Morrin Centre), Quebec
MG	Manuscript Group
NA	National Archives, Kew, U.K.
NAS	National Archives of Scotland, Edinburgh
RG	Record Group
RGO	Registers, General Officers, British Army, 1770–1850
SB	Succession Books, National Archives, Kew, U.K., WO 25
vol	volume
WLCL	William L. Clements Library, Ann Arbor, Michigan
WO	War Office Papers, National Archives, Kew, U.K.

Note on Typography

Where a name in the text is set in small capitals (e.g., JAMES WOLFE), it indicates that there is an entry for that person in Part Three, Biographical Notes.

In new text we have followed modern practice of not using superscripts in such forms as 2nd, 78th and so on (as opposed to 2nd, 78th, etc.). However, we have kept these forms in material from Thompson's letter-books.

INTRODUCTION

One of the most interesting personal accounts of a Highlander who soldiered in North America during the Seven Years' War is found in an old letter-book now in the possession of the Bibliothèque et Archives nationales du Québec (BAnQ) and another similar book held by the Stewart Museum in Montreal. Scrawled in ink, in a sometimes difficult-to-read copperplate script, are the stories and colourful anecdotes of Grenadier Sergeant James Thompson, who served in His Majesty's 78th Regiment of Foot (Fraser's Highlanders). An astute observer with an eye for a humorous story or yarn, the young Highlander, by war's end, was a veteran of Louisbourg, 1758, the Plains of Abraham, 1759, and the less well known battle of Sillery outside Quebec, 1760.

As the 78th Foot was being raised in 1757, Thompson, a native of Tain, near Inverness, nurtured aspirations of being a junior officer. The commander of the grenadier company of Fraser's Highlanders, Charles Baillie, was his best friend, but this connection was not enough to secure him one of the scarce commissions eagerly sought by the disenfranchised Jacobite gentry of the Highlands. Many of the latter were hoping that service in the Georgian king's army would restore their good name and help in recovering their estates, confiscated as punishment for their participation on the losing side of the 1745 uprising.

Thompson thus enrolled as a "gentleman volunteer" in the ranks with the understanding that his friend would actively recommend him for the first vacant officer's commission when it became available and, until that time, he would serve as a sergeant in the grenadier company. Unfortunately, Thompson's mentor and protector was one of the first killed at the Louisbourg landings in 1758, and all hopes of preferment died with Baillie.

Who then was James Thompson of the 78th Foot, and why is his story different from that of any other redcoat in the Georgian army that served in North America during the Seven Years' War? First of all, accounts by a member of the rank and file from this period are very rare. While officers' journals, diaries and letters are fairly commonplace, a perspective of the French and Indian War seen from the ranks is invaluable. This remarkable collection of personal anecdotes by James Thompson concerning some of the key battles and sieges that shaped the future of the North American continent brings to life the frontline experiences of the Highland soldier as seen from the battle and siege lines, as well as from the daily routine of camp or garrison life. Of particular interest are his descriptions of encounters with Indians, his friends in the ranks, his officers, fellow Freemasons and the *Canadien* habitants and American families that he subsequently came to know.

The title of our collection of late 18th-century and early 19th-century anecdotes, "A Bard of Wolfe's Army," was chosen with care. This young Gaelic-speaking soldier who went to the other side of the North Atlantic in 1757 was, in essence, the unofficial regimental bard of the Fraser Highlanders – a bard in that he kept the exploits of his friends, Highland kinsmen and clansmen alive forevermore in his stories. Thus James Thompson was more important than just a sergeant of grenadiers or a teller of stories. Though not officially on the establishment as such, he was a throwback to the age of true clan regiments, a vestige of the ancient Celtic bards, who during battles acted as heralds and walked with immunity between the warring septs.

In earlier times, a bard would have sat at the right hand of the chieftain as his chief advisor and "mouthpiece." In the *Erse* oral culture, bards were the "collective memory" of the clan, the principal repository for the clan's history and genealogy, which included every treaty, alliance and land transaction going back to the mists of time. More than herald, historian, lawyer and storyteller, the bard was the composer of new songs, weaving the living clansfolk into their clan's past legacy and future fortunes. Thus a bard's inclusion of a clansman's name in a song or story was life-changing. Not only did it place him into the oral history of his kinsmen forever, but it clothed a man with honour for the rest of his waking life. No small matter in the Highlands, where the worst Gaelic curse one could bestow upon another person was: "May your name be forgotten forever."

As Thompson advanced in years, his renown as a storyteller was legendary. In January 1827, three years before Thompson's death at the age of ninety-seven, Lord Dalhousie, Quebec's thirteenth governor, wrote:

> Old Thompson dined with me today, with two of his sons.... Of course the conversation was all upon Wolfe, and the same clear recollection of the old man told his stories in the very same words he has always told them so very clear that I sat down before I went to bed to write one or two of his long ones.[1]

Some of the oral anecdotes that his son James Jr. transcribed found their way into local newspapers of the day or were formally published as several monographs in 19th-century historical society papers and transactions. These latter transcriptions have appeared as fragments and segments in subsequent books

---

1. Dalhousie Journal, LAC, Microfilm A-536. (See list of abbreviations, page xiv.)

on the Seven Years' War, starting with Francis Parkman in 1884, but never has Thompson's entire collection of stories spanning his lifetime been published in one volume.

We have structured "Bard..." into three parts. In Part One, we provide a detailed biographical essay of the man, his family and the turbulent times in which he lived, culled from a multitude of sources, including: James Thompson's memoirs and journals; the Canadian War Museum; Library and Archives Canada; the McCord Museum; the National Archives of Scotland; the Literary and Historical Society of Quebec; turn-of-the-century literary works; BAnQ; the Tain & District Museum Trust; Masonic archives; and contemporary newspapers.

Part Two contains all his anecdotes we have collated from a smaller number of sources: the previously mentioned manuscript letter-book held at BAnQ; a recently-discovered (September 2009) manuscript letter-book of James Thompson's anecdotes found in a private collection and now in the possession of the Stewart Museum; a mid-19th century historical work; and an article published in the *Star and Commercial Advertiser* on 16 April 1828.[2] The vast majority of the anecdotes in Part Two come from the letter-book held at BAnQ.

In 1828 James Thompson Jr. started to record his father's anecdotes. The following note clearly explains the process:

> The following memoirs are collected from written statements and oral communications during my residence in the year 1828-9 at my father's house, in Quebec; those acquired through the medium of conversation had previously been imprinted on my mind over many years of repeated recital in my younger days, but not in such a connected manner as to have enabled one to commit the details to writing. The period of my residence with him, being the first year of my being placed on half pay, I found myself so much at leisure as to be enabled to take notes immediately after each recital, and as my father frequently recurred to the same "stories," I had an opportunity afforded me of correcting any circumstance which had been mis-stated, and of introducing particulars that had been omitted. These notes were kept on separate sheets of paper, in order to admit of correction and revision.[3]

On his father's death in August 1830, and recognizing the intrinsic value of his father's oral "war stories," James Jr. started the time-consuming process of gathering the loose sheets and notes and transcribing them into two bound foolscap letter-books, each simply identified on the binding edge with the words "PRIVATE JOURNAL." One letter-book held Anecdotes 1 to 26 (Volume 1), and

---

2. The latter two works are: Alfred Hawkins, *Picture of Quebec: with Historical Recollections* (Quebec, 1834), 395–6; and "Anecdote of Wolfe's Army – History of Sergeant Allan Cameron" in the *Star and Commercial Advertiser,* 16 April 1828.
3. JTC.

the other held Anecdotes 27 to 42 (Volume 2). Once again, the process is clearly explained by the words of James Jr.:

> The bereavement which the family has recently experienced in that Dispensations of Providence which has called him hence, renders these little anecdotes doubly valuable. In the view, therefore, to give them a more comparatively secure form, I have thought it a subject well worthy my attentions to transcribe the contents of the loose papers adverted to, and which I accordingly have commenced at my residence at the village of the Cedars in Lower Canada [today's Côteau-du-Lac], this sixth day of September 1830.[4]

As outside interest in Thompson's anecdotes grew in the 1840s, James Thompson Jr. was repeatedly asked for copies. Hand-copying was a tedious business and as the demand grew, it is surmised that James Thompson Jr. decided to produce a "public" copy of the anecdotes, one which could be loaned out to interested parties. But to satisfy 19th-century sensibilities, a few anecdotes needed to be deleted: those deemed not suitable for public consumption (because they were slightly risqué or contained private family information). Thus, Anecdotes 27, 28, 39, 40 and 41 were removed.[5]

When James Thompson Jr. died in December 1869 without issue, all of his possessions (including his father's journals, letter-books, correspondence, etc., known collectively as the James Thompson collection)[6] were passed down to his nephew, James Thompson Harrower.[7] In 1880 the Harrowers decided to put this material (and other Thompson memorabilia) up for sale. The two-volume "private" letter-books were sold to a private collector or antiquarian book dealer, while the single-volume "public" letter-book (and the rest of the James Thompson collection) was purchased by the Literary and Historical Society of Quebec.[8]

---

4. *Ibid.*
5. This would explain the missing anecdotes in the "public" letter-book now held at BAnQ.
6. The complete collection of James Thompson's papers – memoirs, letters, anecdotes, journals, statistics, etc. – consists of nine bound volumes in total, five of them of folio size, comprising upwards of 2,000 pages. The complete collection of James Thompson Junior's papers – memoirs, letters, etc. – consists of twelve bound volumes in total, all of them of folio size (one volume, number 2, is missing). James Thompson Junior's papers, known collectively as the James Thompson Junior Fonds, was acquired by BAnQ in 1972 (P254, 1972-00-085) and also includes a temperature journal, music manuscripts, correspondence notebooks, and two albums of family papers.
7. James Thompson Harrower was the son of Anne Thompson, Sergeant Thompson's eldest daughter, who married Robert Harrower. See Part Three for Biographical Note for Anne Thompson.
8. In the late 1860s, a number of anecdotes were copied for J.-M. Lemoine, then president of the LHSQ, so the historical importance of the collection was well known to the society.

In 1924 the James Thompson collection was deposited at BAnQ, including the "public" letter-book, and it was eventually purchased outright in 1941. More recently, microfilm copies of the collection were obtained by Library and Archives Canada in Ottawa, as well as the Stewart Museum.

The "public" letter-book at BAnQ has two labels affixed to the front cover:

> James Thompson, Sr.
> Reminiscences
> Recorded by his Son,
> James Thompson, Jr.
>
> Documents, Letters &
> Anecdotes
> Relating to
> Lord Nelson in Quebec
> 1782

The upper label is handwritten and clearly affixed to the cover at a later date (by James Thompson Jr.), while the lower label is permanent, having been affixed to the cover by the manufacturer of the letter-book. This suggests that James Thompson Jr., then on half pay as a retired deputy commissary general in Quebec, had access to an old, unused, letter-book (about sixty years old) which was originally intended for use when Lord Horatio Nelson visited Quebec in 1782. This has caused confusion as some modern archivists have added the lower label to the archival record, not realizing that its contents bear no relationship whatsoever to Lord Nelson's 1782 visit.

The pages of this letter-book are numbered consecutively. Also, each anecdote has been numbered, in red ink, from 1 to 42. However, there are two gaps in the anecdotes without a corresponding gap in the page numbering (obviously the page numbering was added later, perhaps by a reference archivist): Anecdote 26 is followed by Anecdote 29, indicating that Anecdotes 27 and 28 are missing; and Anecdote 38 is followed by Anecdote 42, indicating that Anecdotes 39, 40 and 41 are missing. With the recent discovery of one of the original Thompson letter-books, these "missing" anecdotes are now part of the historical record and are included in this publication.

Only the first twenty-eight anecdotes cover Thompson's service with the 78th Foot (Fraser's Highlanders) over the period 1757–63. The remaining anecdotes (29-42) cover Thompson's experiences as the Overseer of Works for the fortified city of Quebec, including his experiences during the American War of Independence (29).

The editors believe that the recently discovered letter-book is volume two of the original "private" set of letter-books transcribed by James Thompson Jr. in

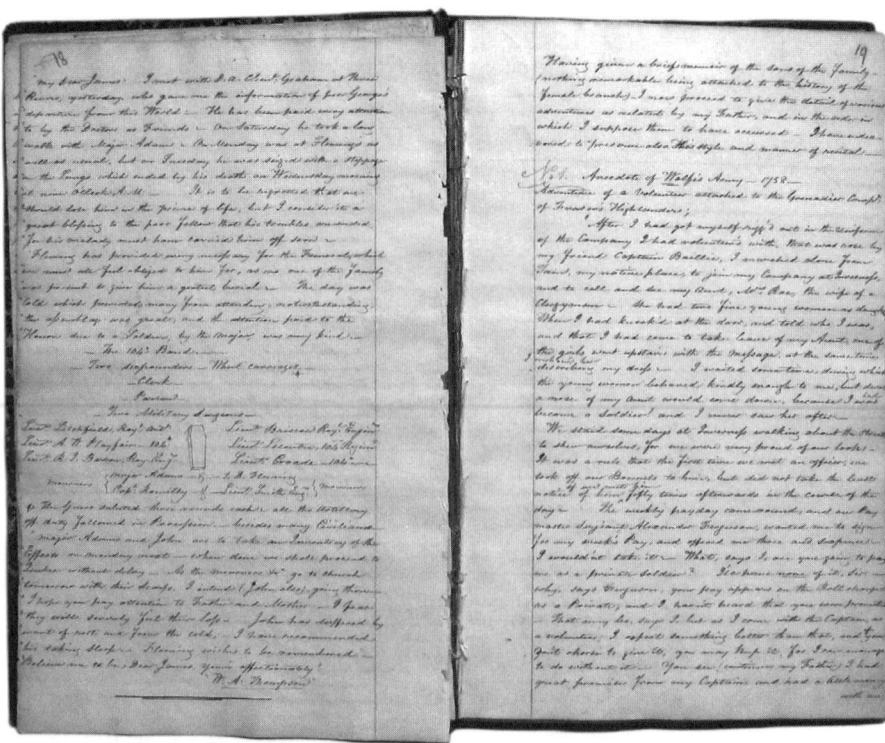

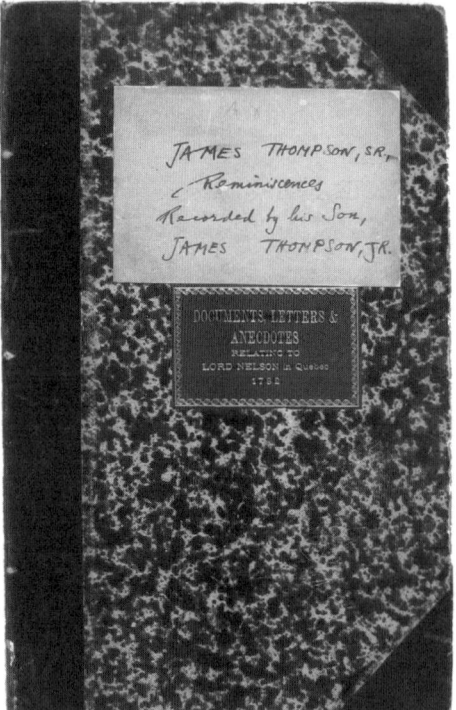

James Thompson's letter-books. (Above and left) The interior and front cover of the letter-book at the Bibliothèque et Archives nationales du Québec. (Below) Damage where pages have been cut from the letter-book now in the collection of the Stewart Museum, Montreal.

1830.⁹ It consists of 177 unnumbered pages. As in the "public" letter-book, each anecdote has been numbered in red ink. The content begins with the last few paragraphs of Anecdote 26 and continues to the end of Anecdote 43.¹⁰ There are three missing leaves, neatly cut out by persons unknown, consisting of six pages of text. This has resulted in the loss of the final paragraphs of Anecdote 29, the entire contents of Anecdotes 30, 31 and 32, and the beginning paragraphs of Anecdote 33. Fortunately, the missing text can be found in the "public" letter-book held at BAnQ. The editors believe that the purchaser of the "private" letter-books also acquired two personal items belonging to James Thompson – his grandmother's silver cup, and his snuff mull. These items are the subject of two of Thompson's anecdotes, Anecdote 30 and 32. Attaching greater value to the silver cup and snuff mull, and knowing the significance of providing the all-important provenance, our unknown collector decided to remove three leaves from Volume 2 of the letter-book, those containing Anecdotes 30 and 32 (which by necessity also included Anecdote 31).

The most recently-discovered letter-book (volume two of the original "private" set), which has been purchased by the Stewart Museum from Mr. James Dinan of Quebec City, has permitted us to publish Thompson's anecdotes in their entirety. This letter-book was discovered in the early 1950s by the Dinan family, who have no connection to Thompson or his descendants. In March 1972 Thompson's silver cup and snuff mull were donated to the McCord Museum in Montreal, along with the three missing leaves from Volume 2 of the "private" journal.¹¹

Over the years, a number of selections from the Thompson collection were published by the Literary and Historical Society of Quebec. One manuscript journal, covering the period from April 1759 to 18 September 1759, was published in its entirety under the lengthy title *A Short Authentic Account of the Expedition against Quebec in the Year 1759, under Command of Major-General James Wolfe: By a Volunteer upon That Expedition.* Originally attributed to James Thompson, it is now believed to have been written by Major Patrick Mackellar, the engineer-in-chief with Wolfe's expedition to Quebec. This mistaken attribution appears to have been started back in the mid-1830s with Thompson's son, who found a manuscript copy of Mackellar's journal written in his father's hand. As it was not

---

9. This suggests that there is another letter-book of James Thompson yet undiscovered: Volume 1, which contains the first 26 anecdotes. It is also possible that copies of the two-volume private letter-books were produced for other family members.
10. Anecdote 43 covers James Thompson Jr.'s private memoirs when he acted as deputy commissary general during the 1837 Lower Canada Rebellion. The addition of this anecdote strongly supports our contention that this volume was originally part of the original "private" set belonging to James Thompson Jr.
11. James Thompson Fonds, McCord Museum, P670.

attributed to Wolfe's chief engineer at that time, James Jr. presumed it was written by his father – although he did note that it was "not in the *usual* mode of my Father's recitation." The error was then repeated by the society's editor when the journal was first published in 1872.[12]

In the process of collecting the anecdotes we also tracked down many of Thompson's surviving personal artefacts, including his broadsword and dirks (Canadian War Museum), his snuff mull and silver thistle cup (McCord Museum) and his infamous war trophy of many years, General Richard Montgomery's sword (Smithsonian Institution). The Quebec house that he built over the period 1791 to 1800 still stands, a designated historic site and present-day bed and breakfast.

Many of the stories Thompson would recount to his listeners over the decades merged into one another. An example of Thompson mixing his stories in Part Two is Anecdote 14, which actually occurs in two different geographic locations in two different years. These "unions" probably occurred when Thompson's memory started to fail him later in life when transcription occurred, or his son James in transcribing the stories left out a paragraph or a missing page. Suffice it to say, the flow of the stories in their original order can be confusing to someone unfamiliar with the regiment's history, campaigns and travels in North America.

Therefore in Part Two, the narrative does not follow the sequence of the anecdotes but instead places them into chronologically structured chapters. Thompson's various tales and recollections that appear throughout the various anecdotes have been moved backwards or forwards into the respective chapters for ease of comprehension. Introductory paragraphs have been added to provide all-important context.[13]

While the anecdotes are written in a storytelling vernacular with a simple straightforward style, the language is, in parts, quaint and the spelling (or his son's spelling) of proper names is sometimes inaccurate. Since everything in Thompson's memoirs, especially his "anecdotes of Wolfe's army," occurred before 1830, we have not hesitated to occasionally – and silently – modernize the punctuation to make the meaning clearer. Thus "Invernefs" becomes "Inverness," "drefs" becomes "dress" and "mefsage" becomes "message." We have

---

12. See, Anon., *The Authorship of a Journal on the Siege of Quebec, in the year 1759* (Quebec, 1872). This publication, prepared by an anonymous associate member of the LHSQ, proves beyond any reasonable doubt that the journal was written by Major Patrick Mackellar.
13. For those interested in seeing Thompson's anecdotes in their original form, see Appendix B, "Anecdote numbers vs page numbers." This list will enable the reader to reconstruct the anecdotes in their original sequence.

left commonly used 18th-century abbreviations, such as "knoc'd" ("knocked") and "rigg'd" ("rigged") as these are fairly obvious. However, we have changed "dev'l" to "devil" as this is not so obvious, and James Jr. used both forms. With the names of people, we have retained the spelling as used by James Jr. with the occasional correction noted within square parentheses. With the names of streets and places, we have kept them in the English form Thompson used – St. Ursula Street instead of rue Sainte-Ursule, Palace Street instead of côte du Palais.

In preparing the footnotes, the editors have kept in mind the needs of the general reader rather than the scholar, though a basic knowledge of the war is assumed on the part of every reader. For the sake of brevity we generally do not footnote our footnotes, but we do cite references for those readers wishing further details and up-to-date scholarship on certain battles, campaigns or aspects of the British army that appear in the book. We also occasionally cite other people's first-hand accounts of the same incidents described by Thompson to provide additional context and, in some cases, to corroborate or expand upon his own memory of the event.

A rule of thumb in our footnoting in Parts One and Two was to briefly identify places, things, foreign words and unfamiliar 18th-century terms at the bottom of the page for immediate reference. This was the lesser of two evils, as requiring the reader to turn to endnotes, we believed, would disrupt the flow and the reader's enjoyment of the narrative. To save space, we placed biographical notes on people mentioned in the text in Part Three, a move that allowed us to include additional contextual detail of the time and, more importantly, connect that person back to the events depicted by Thompson.

Two appendices contain information that has a definite place in the book but could not be placed in the earlier parts. Appendix A contains Thompson's personal memorandum on his career, found in his papers, a key foundation document (also annotated as Anecdote 38 in the letter-books), which we took as our starting point for Part One. Appendix B consists of a table showing the original anecdotes complete with their original titles and in their original order. This will serve as an index to anyone wishing to see how the anecdotes were initially transcribed, titled and sequenced by James Thompson Jr. before our 21st-century editing. Only the oral histories of James Thompson Sr. were included in Part Two.

The editors' principal aim in this project has been to make this rare collection of valuable oral histories heard once again by making it available to both the general public and scholars alike. Now readers can enjoy Thompson's unique perspective on the events and the personalities that shaped the French and Indian War and American Revolution. We hope the "Bard of Wolfe's Army," James

Thompson, a faithful servant of the King, a gallant Highland soldier in the saga that was the Conquest of Canada, and the father of a large and respectable family that played an important part in the early history of the colony, would approve of our humble efforts.

EARL JOHN CHAPMAN
Montreal

LT. COL. IAN MACPHERSON MCCULLOCH
Toronto

St. Andrew's Day, 2010

PART ONE

A Plan of the City of Quebec, the Capital of Canada. Engraved by Thomas Jeffreys in 1760 and published in a book of maps, the map detail shown here highlights buildings and fortifications on the "St. Laurence or the Great River called by the Indians Hoshelaga or Canada River." (David Rumsey Map Collection 4796.002)

A "BROTHER SOLDIER..." JAMES THOMPSON AND THE WOLFE LEGACY

"Be of good cheer, brother Soldier!" Oh! he was a noble fellow! and he was so kind and attentive to our men, that they would have gone thro' fire and water to have serv'd him....

James Thompson, Anecdotes of Wolfe's Army

A short man with windswept white hair was standing on the shore of a cove the French called Anse au Foulon, watching intently as the boatload of Highlanders pulled for the beach in the early morning sunlight. The trees behind him on the steep slopes running up to the Plains of Abraham were already starting to turn red and gold, evidence that early frosts and cold nights had started the seasonal cycle early this year on the lower reaches of the St. Lawrence River.

The man could hear the soldiers talking and the occasional oath uttered as one of them missed a stroke in the pewter-grey waves of the river. As he waited quietly for them to close with the shore, he noted their scarlet coats with buff facings, the brick-red plaids attached to the left shoulder and their muskets ready to hand, upright in their boat. They wore blue bonnets scrugged down against the early morning chill, each headdress sporting a tuft of combed black bear fur that ran from the left side of the bonnet to the crown in the centre. Each time a morning breeze caressed the boat then rippled out along the expanse of river, the black tufts would flutter like feathers.

The prow of the boat was soon crunching into the gravelly beach and the first two Highlanders jumped over the thwarts, their white knees flashing and their shoe buckles sparkling in the sun. Each sported a Highland broadsword on his left hip, and as they pulled and tugged on the boat's painter, the rowers aboard used their oars to pole the boat forward onto dry ground. The watching man noted they were all young men, fit and in their prime, none older than twenty-five years of age. When they were all ashore they finally noticed him and he smiled at them. "Who are you?" he asked in English and "What are you doing here at this hour in the morning?"

"A rehearsal, sir," said the sergeant in charge politely. "It's the 12th of September today and we're getting ready for tomorrow's 250th anniversary of the Battle of the Plains of Abraham up there." The Highlander pointed up the wooded slopes to where the Plains of Abraham once lay, now crisscrossed by innumerable roads and paths, dotted with monuments, ballparks and gardens, all bordered now by the 19th-century urban overspill of the ancient fortified city of Quebec. "The ceremonies will start down here first today though with our museum director and staff, the officers of the various Fraser garrisons and one of our pipers present. Afterwards we'll be going up top for a plaque ceremony."

"Ah," said the man, "would you be Fraser's Highlanders then?"

"Indeed we are sir," said the polite young sergeant in a surprised voice. "Didn't think many people up this way had ever heard of us."

"Oh yes," said the gentleman. "When's your ceremony start again lad?"

"One hour, sir."

"Then I'll be back then, I have something your people will be very interested in."

The man turned away and started walking back along the road that led from the shoreline then curved abruptly up the hillside following the natural contours of the cliffs where once a dirt track had been used by Wolfe's army to haul their guns up on that fateful day of battle in 1759.

The man named Jim Dinan, an Irish immigrant whose family came to Canada at the end of the Second World War, returned as promised. In his hands he carried an old calfskin-bound journal, which, when opened, revealed page after page of tidy copperplate script.

"I think this man James Thompson was in your unit 250 years ago," said Mr. Dinan with a smile and held out the journal to the Adjutant of the Fraser's Highlanders. The former director of the Stewart Museum, Bruce Bolton, immediately sent out a messenger to find Earl Chapman, one of the two editors of this book, who was standing nearby.

On seeing the journal and what it contained, Earl was struck nearly speechless. The last five missing anecdotes of James Thompson's forty-plus oral histories had just appeared out of nowhere. Even more incredible was that they were appearing on today of all days, 12 September 2009, just one day short of the commemoration of the Fraser's Highlanders exploits and achievements at Quebec over two centuries ago.

A serendipitous moment. One of James Thompson's "private" letter-books is shown to surprised members of the re-raised 78th Fraser Highlanders by James Dinan (far right) at the Anse au Foulon on 12 September 2009. Recently acquired by the Stewart Museum in Montreal, this volume contains the five anecdotes missing from the "public" letter-book held at Bibliothèque et Archives nationales du Québec. (Editor's Collection)

As Earl would later relate: "It was almost as if the ghost of Thompson was waiting for us on that beach, 250 years after he had crossed it himself to become part of Canadian history. Those missing few stories revealed on that day had eluded us for the last two years and we were resigned to the fact that they had probably disappeared forever. But not so! The Bard of Wolfe's Army, James Thompson, was marching along with us every step of the way to ensure that all his stories would be published; that the deeds and derring-do of the 78th would live forevermore!"

On 25 August 1830 James Thompson passed away in the family residence on St. Ursula Street in Quebec City. He was in his ninety-eighth year. His death entry in the St. Andrew's Church register recorded for all time that he "belonged to a Highland Regiment which formed part of General Wolfe's Army at the taking of Quebec," in spite of the fact that Thompson's military service had ended some sixty-seven years prior to his death. His death, like the better part of his life, could not shake his short association with James Wolfe, the hero of Quebec.

James Thompson[1] was born 13 March 1733 in the Royal Burgh of Tain, Ross-shire, to James Thomson and his wife, Barbara Stronach.[2] James would, in later life, add the letter "p" to his name at the suggestion of his company commander while crossing to North America, who "considered it the more correct mode of spelling it," but this convention was never adopted by the family in Scotland.

Lack of detailed 18th-century parish records has made it difficult to piece together the details of his immediate family. However, we do know that he had eleven brothers, one of whom was William, born in 1715, and three sisters, Christian, Barbara and Janet, all born in the 1720s. Most of his brothers "served their Country in some Military Capacity in different quarters of the World."[3] James must have been one of the youngest of the children as his father, born in 1672, was sixty-one years of age at the time of his birth.[4]

James Thomson senior was a familiar figure in Tain, prominent during the 1720s as the Presbyterian kirk officer, a responsible and respected position. Kirk officers often lived next to the graveyard, which may be a clue to where the Thomsons' house was located. Thomson's varied duties included maintenance of the kirk and graveyard, keeping out unruly children and vagabonds and announcing funerals. An important part of his job was to help ensure that the congregation observed the Sabbath, attended services regularly and were discouraged from bad behaviour such as drunkenness and fornication. Nobody was exempt from this scrutiny, even the landed gentry, nor from being called to account if their behaviour warranted it.

Sometime later, James Thomson senior shows up as a "shoemaker burgess." The term burgess implied a high standing in the Royal Burgh, suggesting that he was a shoe manufacturer or distributor, rather than just a simple cobbler. Another good indication of his high standing in the community was that impor-

---

1. For consistency and clarity throughout, James Thompson's surname is spelled with a "p" in this monograph, though when he left Tain, he was still a Thomson. This addition to his name while transiting the Atlantic in 1757 may have been an Anglophilic or pro-government statement.
2. No record of Thompson's birth survives in Tain. However, at dinner with the governor general of Canada on 7 January 1827 in Quebec near the end of his life, Thompson specifically mentioned that he would be ninety-four on 13 March of that year. Therefore he was born 13 March 1733. George Ramsay, 9th Earl of Dalhousie Fonds, LAC, MG24-A12, Microfilm A-536. For an edited version see Marjory Whitelaw, ed., *The Dalhousie Journals* (Ottawa, 1978-82), 82 (hereafter Whitelaw, *Dalhousie Journals*).
3. Memorial, James Thompson Jr. to Lord Dalhousie, Cedars, 28 August 1820, LAC, RG8 "C" Series, Microfilm C-2859. James was requesting a land grant for a small island opposite the village of Cedars. This application was rejected.
4. Much of this information on Thompson's family and his early life in Tain comes from Estelle Quick, *James Thompson: A Highlander in Quebec* (Tain & District Museum Trust, 2009). Ms Quick has kindly consented to our use of this material.

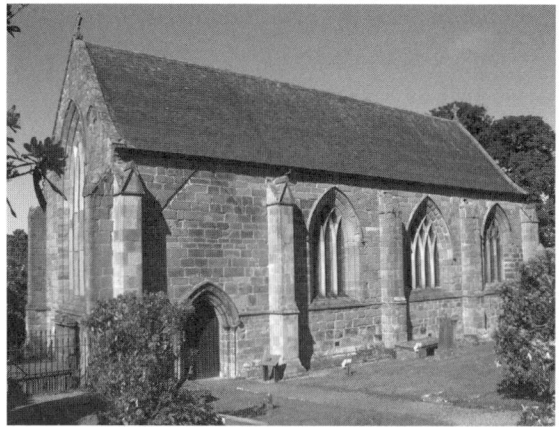

St. Duthus's Collegiate Church, Tain. Located in the centre of Tain, St. Duthus's (above) was built in 1360 and converted to a Collegiate Church by James III in 1487. James Thompson's father served as a kirk officer for Tain and his family attended church services here. The minister, Henry Munro, was married to a Thomson but no family connection has been established at this time. St Duthus's remained as the parish church until 1815 when it was finally abandoned and allowed to fall into decay. Restored in 1877, it is now maintained as a heritage site.

Tain Tolbooth. This multi-purpose building (right), which served as jail, sheriff's office and law court, was built by Alexander Stronach, James Thompson's maternal grandfather, over the period 1706–33. It remains one of Tain's most distinctive landmarks. (Both photos courtesy: Morag Ross Bremner, Tain, Scotland)

tant people witnessed the baptisms of his three daughters.[5] These things suggest that the large Thomson family had some means. As a result, Thompson probably received the best education that his parents could provide, likely attending the grammar school in Tain. At this period, there would have been only one schoolmaster and one's breadth of education depended on the subjects in which the schoolmaster was best versed. An inventory of the books belonging to the Tain schoolmaster who died in 1711 gives an idea of the subjects that were covered: Greek, Latin, mathematics, logic, ethics, history and French. At this time, Gaelic was the language of the ordinary people of Tain, and it would have been Thompson's first language, although he learned to read and write English, a skill that would prove useful later in his military career.

The Thomson family would have attended church services at St. Duthus's

---

5. Old parish registers, Tain.

Collegiate Church.[6] The minister at that time was Hugh Munro, who had previously been minister of nearby Tarbat. His first wife's surname was Thomson, a relatively uncommon name in the area, but there are no records to show whether she was related to Thompson's immediate family.

Thompson's grandmother on his father's side was Jeannot McKulloch (Janet McCulloch), whose brother was a baillie[7] of Dornoch. But it is Thompson's family on his mother's side who are of particular interest, because of the influence they may have had on his later career. His mother, Barbara, was the daughter of Alexander Stronach, a master stonemason and kirk elder from Tarbat and patriarch of a family of masons. Stronach worked on many local buildings during the early part of the 18th century, and between 1706 and 1733 he designed and built Tain's new and unusual tolbooth, which housed the town's constabulary, court offices and jail. Although the tolbooth was finished by the time Thompson was born, it stood, and still stands today, as a prominent demonstration of his grandfather's expertise.[8] As a young man, Thompson must have worked with his uncles and cousins, learning the skills he was to use later in Quebec.[9]

We know that Thompson was tall and well built as he was later described as "a big giant" by his friends in Quebec.[10] His own memoirs[11] recount feats of

---

6. Located in the centre of Tain, St. Duthus's was built in 1360 by William, Earl of Ross. In 1487 James III had it converted to a Collegiate Church. It was the parish church until 1815 when it was abandoned and allowed to fall into decay. It was restored in 1877 and is now maintained for monumental and memorial purposes. In Thompson's day there were external staircases with entrances through the windows leading to lofts built to accommodate the growing congregation. These additions were removed when the church was restored.
7. A baillie was a local civic officer in Scottish burghs, equivalent to the post of alderman or magistrate in other countries.
8. Stronach's tolbooth remains Tain's most distinctive building. First built in 1630 to house court offices and a jail, as well as to collect tolls and taxes from traders. During the Highland clearances, it was used as an administrative centre. An engraved stone from the previous tolbooth is set into the central turret. It reads: THIS WARK BEGIT 1631 JHON MACKULLOCH BEING PROVOST.
9. In view of Thompson's later employment by the Engineers Department at Quebec, this connection cannot be a coincidence.
10. J.-M. Lemoine, *Picturesque Quebec: A Sequel to Quebec Past and Present* (Montreal, 1882), 100. Lemoine stated that Judge Henry Black (c.1799–1873), who knew Thompson well, once described him as a "big giant," also adding that he had an "athletic frame." Henry Black was born in Quebec about 1799. He was appointed Judge Surrogate of the Court of Vice Admiralty, and as a reward for his public services he was created a Companion of the Bath. In 1840, he was made a Doctor of Law by Harvard University. Judge Black died in Quebec on 16 August 1873, aged seventy-three.
11. JTC. The James Thompson Fonds, held at BAnQ, consists of a number of journals, diaries, letter-books, etc. Thompson's anecdotes (including his "Anecdotes of Wolfe's Army") are contained in a letter-book entitled "James Thompson, Sr., Reminiscences Recorded by his Son, James Thompson, Jr.," Call Number P450-1960-01-544, Box 4.

strength and endurance, such as carrying a wounded man half a mile without a rest and walking eighty miles in a day. Even if these stories are exaggerated, they suggest a large, strong and active man – he certainly survived considerable physical hardships to live to an active old age.

In 1754 Thompson became a Freemason in his home village, however Tain's Lodge St. Duthus No. 82, the oldest lodge in the county of Ross and Cromarty, did not receive its charter until 2 February 1761. There are no records of any activity before this date, though it is possible that the lodge was operating for a number of years before it received its official charter. In any event, it is likely that Thompson's grandfather, Alexander Stronach, was involved in these early masonic activities.[12]

The Jacobite rising in 1745 brought great upheavals to Easter Ross, the eastern part of the old county of Ross-shire of which Tain was one of the principal towns. With some exceptions, the major families of the area – the Munros, Rosses and Sutherlands – were supporters of the English Crown, unlike the Mackenzies and Frasers to the south. The government's actions following its victory at Culloden in 1746 were swift and ruthless, with troops moving into the Jacobite strongholds killing, burning and looting as they went. The most prominent supporters of the rising were exiled and their estates were sold off or annexed. Some, including SIMON FRASER, Lord Lovat, were eventually executed. In an effort to crush the clan system, the government abolished the Scottish chiefs' rights of jurisdiction and passed a new law, the Act of Proscription, which made it illegal to wear Highland dress or carry arms (the only exception being for soldiers serving in the army). These events "were the backdrop against which James Thompson grew from a boy to a man."[13]

There were also some life changes. Thompson's family was dwindling, his father having died in 1755 at the age of eighty-three after falling down some cellar stairs. His sisters had probably married by 1755 and were bringing up their own families. His older brother William "had gone for a soldier," probably during the Jacobite uprisings, and was now serving as a sergeant in the 1st Foot, stationed in Ireland. By 1756, with the Seven Years' War intensifying, Britain needed ever

---

There are also four large journals that Thompson kept over the period 1779–81 which contain day-to-day details of his work on the fortifications, Call Number P254-1972-00-085/2/3. Within these dry, engineering details are snippets of personal information.

12. "List of the Members of St. Andrew's Lodge, No. 2, Quebec ... 25 October 1789," quoted in Henry Sadler, *Thomas Dunckerley: His Life, Labours and Letters* (Kessinger Publishing, 2003), 54–5. The list comprises seventy names, and Thompson's name appears as the first one as "James Thompson, Overseer of work for Quebec; made a Mason in Scotland in 1754, and admitted a Member on the 20 October 1760; S. Warden of the Lodge when constituted, now Master."

13. Quick, *James Thompson: A Highlander in Quebec*, 3.

more military manpower. William Pitt's new ministry believed that recruiting in the Highlands would produce good soldiers and help to reduce feelings of alienation and disaffection.

Some of the Jacobite supporters who had been in disgrace since 1746 saw an opportunity to re-establish themselves by offering to raise troops from among their clansmen. One such opportunist was Simon Fraser, Master of Lovat and son of the executed Lord Lovat. He was instructed to raise a marching regiment to fight in North America and he was commissioned as its lieutenant colonel commandant early in January 1757. Starting off as the 2nd Highland Battalion of Foot, Fraser's new regiment would be entered into the order of battle as the 63rd Foot, but later renumbered upwards as the 78th. A good portion of the recruitment was done by Simon Fraser himself from the old Lovat estates west of Inverness, but he appointed other Highland gentlemen to recruit companies from the areas around their homes. One of these was CHARLES BAILLIE, previously a second lieutenant in the 21st Foot, who had transferred to the newly-raised 2nd Highland Battalion and was placed in command of the regiment's elite grenadier company.[14]

Charles was the eldest son of William Baillie of Rosehall, the factor for the Balnagowan estates belonging to the Earls of Ross. The Baillies were reasonably eminent Sutherland landowners themselves and certainly part of a totally different social stratum to the Thomsons. However, Charles was about the same age as James Thompson and, according to him, his "best and most intimate friend."[15] It is difficult to explain the 18th-century social structure in the Highlands that enabled Thompson and Baillie to be close friends but it is most likely they became friends at school. According to one observer the various stages of family intermarriage meant that:

> there was scarce an individual, in at least the northern counties, whose claim to self respect was not involved in the honour of some noble family. There ran through his humble genealogy some silver thread of high descent; some great-great-grandfather or grandmother connected him with the aristocracy of the country; and it was his pride and honour, not that he was an independent man, but that he was in some sort a dependent gentleman.[16]

Captain Baillie was responsible for recruiting in and around Tain, and one of the men he recruited was his friend James Thompson. Baillie had promised

---

14. At this time, grenadiers were chosen from the strongest and largest soldiers. By the 19th century, the throwing of grenades, their initial function, was no longer relevant, but grenadiers were still chosen for being the most physically powerful soldiers and would lead assaults on the field of battle.
15. JTC – Anecdote 4.
16. Hugh Miller, *Tales and Sketches* (Edinburgh, 1872), 322.

Thompson that he would be recommended for an officer's commission when a vacancy occurred, and on this basis Thompson accepted the King's shilling and was attested as a volunteer.[17] As it turned out, Baillie was killed the following year during the assault landing at Louisbourg and "did not live to pull the necessary strings to get Thompson a commission."[18]

Because of his imposing size and frame, Thompson was a natural to serve in Baillie's grenadier company, but it seems that he was initially enrolled as a private soldier. As he had "a little money and the promise of a commission from his captain," Thompson proudly refused to accept a private's pay, telling the pay sergeant, "I expect something better than that … you may keep it for I can manage without it."[19] A few days later he was paid as a sergeant, though it is not entirely clear how he was carried on the regimental roster, at least at the beginning of his military career. Certainly the earliest anecdotes indicate he performed the duties of a sergeant, such as being in charge of sick parties, paying and caring for the welfare of the men and so on. Later anecdotes are rife with the names of his fellow sergeants, many from good families. Regardless of his official position within the regiment, Thompson would refer to himself as a "volunteer in Wolfe's army" for the rest of his life.[20]

Marching first across the breadth of Scotland and then along the eastern shore of Ireland, Fraser's Highlanders worked their way southwards to Cork, the normal embarkation point for regiments destined for North America. On 1 July 1757, troop transports carrying Fraser's Highlanders raised anchor and sailed for Halifax, Nova Scotia. According to historian John Houlding, it normally took two to three years for a newly raised regiment to reach the status of "fit for service."[21] The Fraser Highlanders that embarked from Cork were a "raw, undisciplined set," according to Thompson, as they had been raised a mere six

---

17. It is possible that Thompson enlisted as a "gentleman volunteer," the 18th-century approximation of an officer cadet. He certainly had the necessary qualifications for a commission, if not the financial means. The regiment did carry a number of gentleman volunteers but these were usually drawn from those with higher social connections.
18. Ralph J. Harper, *The Fraser Highlanders* (Montreal, 1979), xii.
19. JTC – Anecdote 1.
20. Thompson's son claimed his father "held no rank in the Army." Thompson himself stated that he was a volunteer although technically, every soldier was a volunteer. Thompson also stated that he was "selected to do duty as a sergeant" at Louisbourg, implying that he was a private soldier up to that time. During the Quebec campaign he served as an "acting grenadier sergeant" and as a "hospital sergeant," and in 1763 the regiment's disbandment muster lists him as a grenadier sergeant. Describing himself as a volunteer, particularly in his later years in Quebec, is understandable as such an undeterminable rank would have a better cachet within the city's snobbish British elite, suggesting Thompson was indeed considered suitable officer material but did not receive a vacancy.
21. John A. Houlding, *Fit for Service: The Training of the British Army 1715–1795* (Oxford University Press, 1981), 295–6.

months earlier and had no field experience.[22] There can be no doubt that they received their advanced training "the hard way, in the field."[23] Even Thompson had no doubt about his regiment's lack of experience, stating on a number of occasions that "they knew nothing about parade exercise, and figuring away with their fuzees...."[24] Fortunately, the regiment would not see action until July 1758, giving them a year and a half to hone their craft.

Thompson led a charmed life. He survived every major action in which his regiment was engaged without receiving a scratch, including the assault landing and siege of Louisbourg, the rearguard action on the Beauport flats near Montmorency Falls, the siege and capture of Quebec, the battle of Sillery and the capture of Montreal.[25] Starting at Louisbourg, Thompson developed an affection for General JAMES WOLFE, the "soldier's friend," fondly known by the Highlanders as the "red-headed Corporal."[26] This affection was apparently returned by Wolfe, as Thompson would claim in later life that he "received as much attention from him as if he had been a Father to me ... he knew that I was a volunteer."[27]

According to one account, the day before the assault landing at Louisbourg (and his death), Captain Baillie had introduced Thompson to Colonel Fraser:

> From a presentiment of what was to befall him, and motives of pure friendship, this officer, the day previous to the landing, addressed a letter to Colonel Fraser, recommending Mr. Thompson to his protection, and took an opportunity of introducing him to his personal knowledge, thereby securing to him a pledge which throughout all the various services in which the regiment was afterwards engaged, was faithfully redeemed.[28]

---

22. *Ibid.*, 344. Houlding has confirmed the efficacy of camp training. Interestingly, of the forty-six regiments which saw service during the Seven Years' War in North America, the three Highland regiments [2/42nd (Royal Highlanders), 77th (Montgomery's), and 78th (Fraser's)] were the most inexperienced.
23. *Ibid.*, 355. Advanced training consisted of the detailed firings and manoeuvres drawn from the regulations and from customary practice. In North America, they would be practised endlessly, as weather permitted, in both the garrisons and cantonments as the army prepared to take the field in the spring.
24. JTC – Anecdotes 4 and 24.
25. Most of the details of the actions in which the Frasers were engaged have been purposely condensed or eliminated, as the full stories (or at least Thompson's part in them) are covered elsewhere in Thompson's "Anecdotes of Wolfe's Army."
26. JTC – Anecdotes 7 and 10. According to Thompson, this affectionate sobriquet came from "the circumstance that he had red hair, and because he wore an aiguillette similar to the worsted badge of distinction worn by the Corporals of that day."
27. *Ibid.* Once again, the use of the indeterminate term "volunteer" – this reads much better than "he knew that I was a private soldier."
28. "The Late Mr. J. Thompson," *Star and Commercial Advertiser*, 8 September 1830. The obituary editor likely obtained his information from the Thompson family. The Literary and Historical Society of Quebec published this anecdote in its *Transactions*, New Series, No. 22 (1898), under the subheading "Concerning the Journal of James Thompson:

"**A soldier's soldier.**" When news of his heroic death reached Britain on 16 October 1759, General James Wolfe became an overnight celebrity, the public demanding to know what he looked like at the time of his triumph. J.S.C. Schaak's first painting of Wolfe, a full-length portrait executed in 1760, is considered the "best known public image of Wolfe" as it was based on an eyewitness sketch by Wolfe's aide de camp, Captain Hervey Smythe. This bust-length portrait, attributed to Schaak, was executed about 1767 and likely copied from his earlier full-length portrait of the famous general. (National Portrait Gallery)

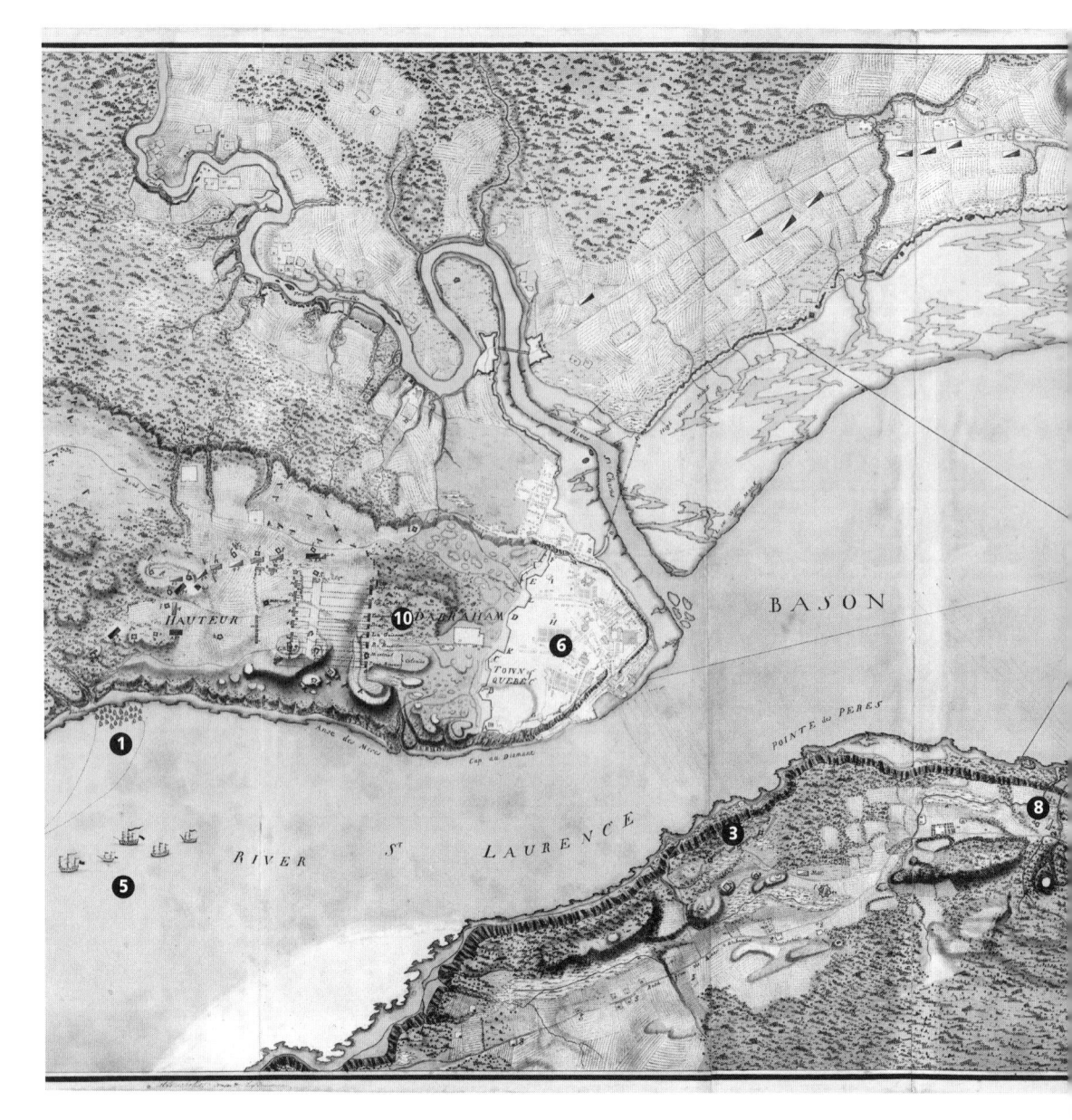

Plan of the Town of Quebec the Capital of Canada in North America … 1759. One of a number of variant examples of Chief Engineer Patrick Mackellar's finely drawn and coloured manuscript maps of Quebec, the map shown here is personally signed by Mackellar and believed to be the master copy. It is a remarkable document, surveyed and drawn by three battlefield participants shortly after the fall of Quebec, in the tradition of battlefield commemoration maps, and was certain to be received with favour – especially if destined for the fine collection of the king's son. Mackellar's team included Captain Hugh Debbig, an experienced and talented member of the engineer corps, and two officers from the 60th Foot – Captain Samuel Holland, seconded as assistant engineer and a Wolfe protégé, one of the most talented and advanced military map-makers in America, and Lieutenant J.W.F. Des Barres, another foreign-born officer, acting as assistant engineer in 1759, perhaps the most talented and competent with his Swiss mathematical education. The Europeans were ahead of the British in mapping skills at the time, and Holland and Des Barres brought cutting-edge knowledge and probably their own personal map-making instruments to America. The map is shown here slightly cropped at both sides. (LAC NMC 21345)

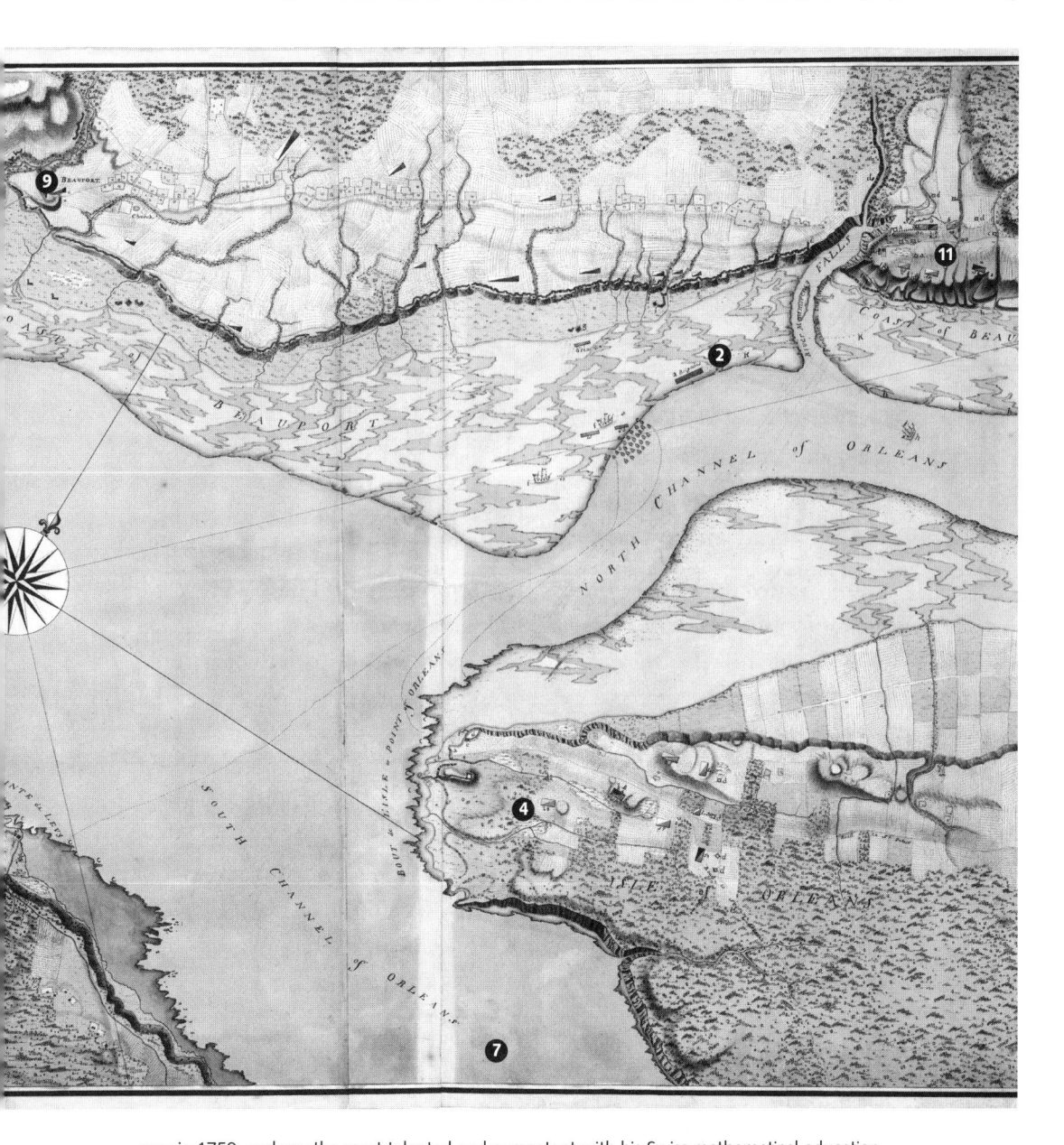

1. Anse au Foulon
2. Attack at Montmorency on 31 July 1759.
3. British batteries at Pointe aux Pere
4. British camp and main hospital on Île d'Orléans
5. British ships which passed Quebec, i.e. *Sutherland, Stork*, etc.
6. Fortified city of Quebec
7. Main British fleet in south channel
8. Moncton's camp at Pointe Lévy
9. Montcalm's HQ at Beauport
10. Plains of Abraham
11. Wolfe's camp at Montmorency

The veracity of this story is suspect however as Colonel Fraser's pledge was never "faithfully redeemed" as claimed and it is doubtful that Thompson needed introduction as both he and the colonel were fellow Freemasons and thus "brethren." Indeed, Thompson implies in at least two of his anecdotes that he enjoyed the especial favour of the colonel due to the latter's Masonic connection rather than to Baillie's efforts.

On the morning of the battle of the Plains of Abraham, a thirty-man detachment of the 78th Foot[29] had been left "on the beach" (the Anse au Foulon). The lack of any anecdotes by Thompson on the actual fighting on the Plains would strongly support the conclusion that, despite all his supposed close association with Wolfe, he was not present on the battlefield when his hero fell in this moment of glory. The editors believe Thompson was left out of battle and was attending to casualty evacuation down at the Anse au Foulon.

Given Thompson's duties on that day — conveying Wolfe's remains to the warship *Royal William*, and his role as a hospital sergeant at Pointe Lévy — he was likely placed in charge of the detachment which secured the landing place and was in place to ensure efficient casualty-evacuation back across the river. Consisting of the regiment's artificers and pioneers, this detachment could have helped clear the wagon track leading to the heights, a job which needed a steady, dependable, take-charge individual, and one with some civil engineering skills — someone like Sergeant James Thompson. When Wolfe's body arrived at the landing place, it was Thompson's lot to "have direction of the party that convey'd his body on board the 64-gun ship of war...."[30] Wolfe's body was taken via St. Joseph's Church at Pointe Lévy, which had been previously converted to a temporary hospital. While here, Wolfe's body was embalmed by Eleanor Job, the wife of an artillery soldier who also acted as a battlefield nurse in what was then called the "flying hospital."[31]

1758–1830." A similar story appeared in another of the Society's publications: Anonymous, *A Short Authentic Account of the Expedition against Quebec in the Year 1759 under Command of Major General James Wolfe: By a Volunteer upon That Expedition* (Quebec, 1872), 41 (wrongly attributed to James Thompson). In this latter version, the story, as related by James Thompson Jr. is a little different: "On the passage to Halifax, Captain Bailley introduced my Father to the Colonel, who promised to use his interest in procuring for him a Commission; but no vacancy having occurred, and the Regiment having been disbanded after the Conquest ... he was left without employment...."

29. The 63rd Foot had been renumbered to the 78th on 21 April 1758.
30. JTC – Anecdote 7.
31. Sylvanus Urban, *The Gentlemen's Magazine*, vol XCIII (London, July–December 1823), 640. Born about 1718, Job came to Canada as one of over 500 women who accompanied Wolfe's army. As she was known to the troops, "Good Mother Job" acted as principal nurse in what was called the "flying hospital" and at Quebec she was detailed to embalm Wolfe's body. At the end of the war she returned to England, ending up as a pauper in the parish of St. Giles. She died on 17 September 1823.

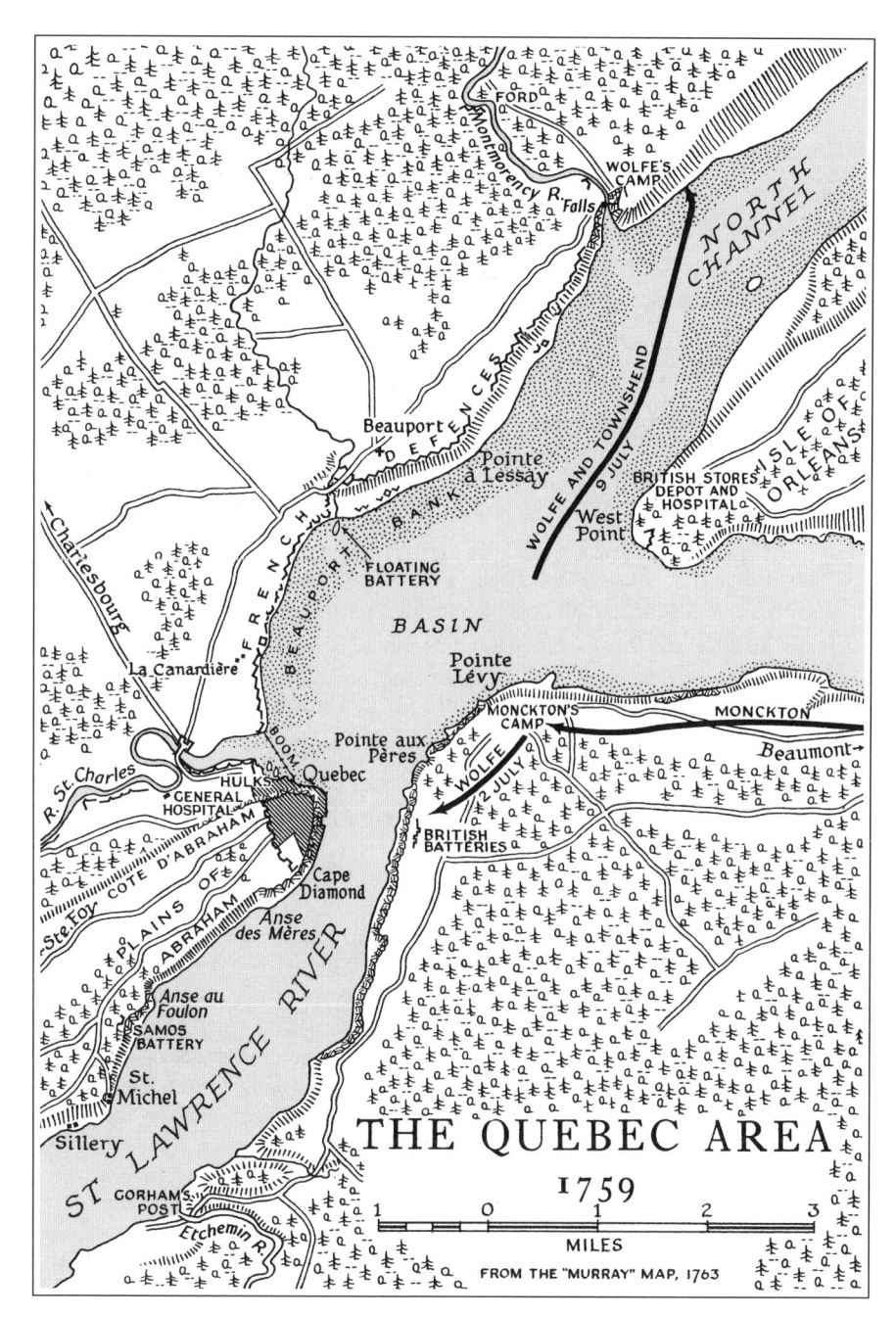

Murray map. The drawing shown here is based on the Quebec portion of General James Murray's "Survey of the Settled Parts of the Colony and the St. Lawrence...," a Canadian cartographic milestone. With the final surrender of the French army at Montreal on 8 September 1760, the British had complete control of the entire St. Lawrence valley and some 65,000 *Canadiens* – yet knew little about the region. What was needed was a map that showed towns, parishes, roads, rivers and fords, as well as terrain features and defensible positions, or as stated by Murray, a map of the St. Lawrence so that the British army would never again "be at a loss how to attack and conquer this country in one campaign." John Montressor, Samuel Holland and William Spry all worked on the project. (Map by C.C.J. Bond from C.P. Stacey, *Quebec, 1759: The Siege and the Battle*)

On 18 September 1759, five days after the battle on the Plains of Abraham, the victorious British army took possession of Quebec, beginning an association between the army and the city's inhabitants that would last 112 years.[32] They found Quebec in a "most ruinous condition," there being "hardly a house in town that was not hurt either by shots or shells, or was habitable without repairing."[33] Based on early surveys, British engineers quickly determined that Quebec's fortifications,[34] while virtually undamaged from the siege and bombardment, were in need of considerable improvements. British engineers stated bluntly that the outer defences

> consisted of little more than the fronts towards the land, were little more than half finished, there being neither ditch, covered way, nor outworks, the scarp wall was seen places from the top .... of the parapet to the foundation. Notwithstanding these, and a variety of other difficulties, it was resolved to keep possession of it, and all possible measures for the security and accommodation of the garrison, were entered upon without delay.[35]

With Britain's financial house in ruinous condition, primarily because of the huge costs of the Seven Years' War, it took many years to bring Quebec's defences up to European standards.[36] This state of affairs, coupled with Thompson's civil engineering skills learned at his grandfather's knee in Scotland, made

---

32. The last British troops marched out of the Quebec Citadel in 1871.
33. Quoted from "Plan of Quebec with the Positions of the British and French Army's [sic] on the Heights of Abraham, 13th September 1759." WLCL, Murray Repetition Map No. 1, Sheet 2.
34. Construction of Quebec's masonry-faced *enceinte* was started in panic not long after the great fortress of Louisbourg fell in 1745 and replaced an earlier system of redoubts and palisades. Protecting the eastward approach from the Plains of Abraham, the new fortifications consisted of six bastions joined by sections of curtain wall. While they were essentially complete by 1759, some important aspects were missing. Post Conquest, the British authorities naturally distrusted the citizens of Quebec and this attitude was expressed in the manner in which they occupied the city. French authorities had integrated their military complexes into the fortifications themselves to facilitate the town's defensive capability. By contrast, the British instituted military complexes in almost every part of the town including the Jesuits' College, the Intendant's Palace, the Nouvelles Casernes (New Barracks) and the Dauphine Barracks, as well as numerous homes (which infuriated the population). This policy would continue into the 19th century when the British constructed the Citadel, the Esplanade, the Royal Engineers Yard, Rampart Road (next to the ramparts) and Artillery Park. In this way, the conquered population was constantly reminded of British military strength, to discourage any attempts at insurrection.
35. Quoted in notes from the "Plan of Quebec with the Positions of the British and French Army's [sic] on the Heights of Abraham, 13th September 1759." WLCL, Murray Repetition Map No. 1, Sheet 2.
36. In fact, the permanent citadel wouldn't be completed until 1831, seventy years after the British had taken Quebec.

"**In a most ruinous condition.**" This was how Wolfe's chief engineer, Major Patrick Mackellar, described Quebec's buildings shortly after its surrender in September 1759, bleakly writing in his journal: "The Buildings in general [are] … infinitely worse than we could have imaged; for besides those burnt, there was hardly a house in the Town that was not injured by either shot or shells nor are they habitable without repairs." This picture shows soldiers of the garrison, including kilted Highlanders of the 78th Foot, climbing the road from Lower Town to Upper Town with the Bishop's Palace at the right. James Thompson would have an apartment in the Palace for several years. Print after Richard Short. (LAC C-041514)

him a valuable resource and ensured that his services would be in demand for the rest of his life.

At this time, the population of the province numbered about 70,000, the majority of which were French-speaking and Roman Catholic.[37] In the 110 rural parishes in Quebec, there was only a scattering of Protestants. As the regiments had their own chaplains accompanying them, Protestant services were held inside the city immediately following the surrender. The first Presbyterian service and subsequent ones were conducted in the city by the 78th Foot's own Reverend ROBERT MACPHERSON. Thompson, a practising Presbyterian, would no doubt have attended these early services.

Another important event occurred on 28 November 1759 when the Freemasons of six regimental "travelling" lodges held the first joint meeting of the Craft

---

37. Wylie Cable Clark, "The Early Presbyterianism of Quebec under Dr. Spark," LHSQ, *Transactions*, New Series, No. 27 (1908).

in Quebec.[38] It is surprising that the Masons were able to hold a meeting under the conditions that prevailed – winter was fast approaching, food and fuel were scarce and over 500 houses had been destroyed by British artillery during the three-month bombardment.

During the first winter within the walls of Quebec, most of Fraser's Highlanders were lodged in the Jesuits' College (later, the Jesuits' Barracks), while Thompson and a few of his men, likely the regiment's "hatchet men" or pioneers, were lucky enough to lodge in a small house "in the lane leading to the Esplanade … although it was scarcely habitable from the number of our shells that had fallen through it."[39] As a sergeant, Thompson was entitled to a little privacy, so with the help of a carpenter named Hector Munro he had a small "cabinet" built in one of the interior corners.[40] With the help of a small wood stove, Thompson and his men passed the winter comfortably enough, in spite of the obnoxious smoke produced by burning green wood.

Over the winter of 1759–60 Thompson was detached[41] to the garrison's Engineer Department, the beginning of a lifelong association with that corps.[42] His first job was to supervise 200 men from the garrison[43] in making fascines[44] in the woods on the north side of the St. Charles River, an "art" that he had learned during the siege of Louisbourg in 1758. The winter of 1759–60 was brutal, even by Quebec standards, and Thompson and his men suffered severely as they were

---

38. John Gawler to unknown recipient, Woolwich, 9 February 1769, quoted in Sadler, *Thomas Dunckerley: His Life, Labours and Letters*, 51–4. Gawler remembers eight or nine lodges, which assembled together and agreed to choose an acting Grand Master to preside over them, "the better to advance Masonry, regulate their proceedings, and unite them in one common band of brotherly love."
39. JTC – Anecdote 23. In 1759 when this incident occurred, this location was pasture land used by cattle belonging to the Ursuline nuns. The Esplanade, a parade ground for garrison troops and volunteer militia, was only laid out between 1779 and 1783.
40. In this context Thompson's "cabinet," or in French *cabinet privé*, was a small room or enclosure built within a larger space. Providing sergeants with a small private room within the soldier's lodging was standard practice in 18th-century British barracks.
41. He would have been "detached" to the Engineers Department from his regiment, and considered "attached" by the engineers for work purposes. When he was locally billeted he would have remained under the administration of the Fraser Highlanders, but if deployed away from his parent unit, he would have been "under command" (or as they termed it in those days, "on command").
42. The Corps of Engineers was formed in 1716 and put under the control of the Board of Ordnance. It became the Corps of Royal Engineers in April 1787. In Canada the Engineers Department was also known as the Civic Department.
43. Thompson's detachment was under the command of a captain and two subalterns – he was the senior non-commissioned officer. Thompson claimed that the men were all from Fraser's Highlanders.
44. Fascines. Sticks bound together in large bundles, used as reinforcement in the construction of earthworks, dikes and ramparts.

dressed only in their "regimental Highland dress."[45] However, Thompson, ever the resourceful soldier, passed the nights comfortably enough as he managed to find a good supply of blankets.

By spring 1760 Thompson's work party had amassed "over 45,500 well-bound fascines made and brought on the men's shoulders."[46] Perhaps Thompson was fortunate in getting this assignment, as the inactive men remaining behind in the garrison suffered severely from sickness and scurvy. Of the grim total of 670 in the Quebec garrison who would perish over the winter, 106 were Highlanders. In April, the Highlanders' muster roll numbered 894 all ranks, with only 314 men considered "fit for duty," the remainder still recovering from wounds or sick.[47]

On 24 June 1760 Colonel Fraser was installed as Provincial Grand Master in Quebec, and on the following 20 October, a lodge in the 78th Foot was established under his Warrant.[48] ALEXANDER LEITH was appointed master, while Thompson was appointed senior warden and acting secretary.[49] Over the period 1759–77 Thompson kept notes of these early meetings, as well as copies of letters written and received by him, and these records have played an important part in establishing the early history of Freemasonry in Quebec.[50]

---

45. JTC – Anecdote 38. Another memorandum appears in a small, bound diary which is more extensive than that found in the "Reminiscences" Letter-book (both held at BAnQ). Quoted passages which follow were taken from both of these memoranda.
46. *Ibid.*
47. "Return of the present State of His Majesty's Forces in Garrison at Quebec, 24 April 1760," NA, CO 5/64, fol. 209. The 106 dead occurred over the period 18 September 1759 to 24 April 1760.
48. Initially numbered No. 6 (eventually No. 211 by the Grand Lodge of England). When Fraser's Highlanders were shipped back to Scotland for disbandment in 1763, it continued as a civilian lodge, adopting the name St. Andrew's Lodge about 1766.
49. Quoted from Pemberton Smith, *Research into Early Canadian Masonry, 1759–1869* (Quality Press, 1939): "Thompson became Master in 1761. His name is repeated six times during this period, many times being re-elected, once holding the office for four successive years. In the term mentioned, Thompson sat in the Master's Chair for thirteen years out of twenty-four. He acted as Secretary for eight of the twenty-four years and went back and helped the lodge by acting as one of the Wardens six times. He replaced William Paxton as Provincial Grand Secretary and faithfully performed these duties for the Provincial Grand Lodge for approximately two decades."
50. Thompson's Masonic note book remained in the family for many years. In 1921 it was reported that an elderly lady had turned it over to a prominent Freemason in Gaspé, claiming that James Thompson had been her grandfather. This book turned out to be a most precious find, since the original transactions of the Provincial Grand Lodge of Canada had been lost to history. In 1926 the Grand Secretary of the Grand Lodge of Quebec took the book with him to London and had it carefully checked against the records of the United Grand Lodge of England. All the London correspondence copied by Thompson into his book was subsequently verified and the book remains as the sole authentic record in Canada of the transactions of the first Provincial Grand Lodge.

Many of Thompson's friends and fellow soldiers were also Freemasons. One of these was Sergeant ALEXANDER "SANDERS" SIMPSON, his cousin and one of his best friends, who also served in the grenadier company of Fraser's Highlanders. After the war, Simpson remained in Quebec and he and his wife (Sarah) opened Simpson's Coffee House on Market Place Street (Place Royale) in Lower Town, a common meeting place for fellow Freemasons. Another good friend and fellow soldier was Sergeant JOHN GAWLER of the Royal Artillery, whom Thompson first met when their respective lodges were being established in Quebec. When Gawler returned to England, he acted as an unofficial representative for his brethren left in Quebec. Thompson and Gawler remained in touch until the latter's death in 1805. So close was the friendship that Thompson named one of his sons after his friend, and when Gawler sent his sons (William and Felix) out to Quebec as young men, Thompson kept an eye on them and paid their bills.

After his first assignment during the winter of 1759–60, Thompson remained "attached" to the Engineers Department, as he later stated, "from this time [winter of 1759–60] and until the Conquest of Canadas was finally secured, my services were chiefly in the field, under the denomination of Clerk of Works...."[51]

He was put under the immediate command of WILLIAM SPRY, Quebec's senior engineering officer, but was reunited with his grenadiers in time for the battle of Sillery on 28 April 1760, when the French army under the Chevalier de Lévis attempted to recapture Quebec. Thompson's company commander, Captain ALEXANDER FRASER of Culduthel, was wounded during the battle and Thompson, acting as a covering sergeant, was forced to "move up into line, which I could not do without my resting one foot on his body."[52]

The battle was fought on almost the same ground as the year before, though slightly more to the west, while the armies' positions were reversed, British facing west and French facing east. Similar to what MONTCALM[53] had done the year before, Brigadier General JAMES MURRAY misread the enemy's intent and came down off a superior position near the Buttes-à-Neveu to try a *coup de main*. It backfired as the French were actually advancing under cover in the Sillery Wood. Murray's tiny army, like Montcalm's the summer before, was beaten and broken in three hours of bloody, obstinate, and often hand-to-hand fighting. The British army, already severely weakened by sickness and scurvy, lost a third of its strength. Murray's exhausted soldiers in their hurried retreat left their shovels and picks on the Buttes-à-Neveu, where they had intended entrenching before the battle.

---

51. JTC – Anecdote 38.
52. JTC – Anecdote 23.
53. Major General Louis-Joseph de Montcalm.

Lévis quickly organized a makeshift siege utilizing the captured British entrenchment tools. He had the advantage of knowing the local terrain best suited to approach the fortified city. He also knew the weakest spots in the defences to batter with his scarce artillery, and soon his purpose-built batteries opened fire on the city and quickly inflicted severe damage on the Glacière Bastion. French hopes for reinforcements from France were dashed four days later when three British ships arrived in the Basin on the evening of 15 May to reinforce a frigate that had already arrived. Lévis was forced to admit that help was not coming and withdrew back to Montreal.

In summer 1760 Murray would advance on Montreal, while simultaneously thrusts were made north along the Lake Champlain–Montreal corridor by Brigadier General William Haviland, while Major General JEFFERY AMHERST and his large army came at Montreal from the west via Oswego–Lake Ontario, then down the St. Lawrence River. Thompson was part of the 242-man detachment of Fraser's Highlanders which advanced with Murray's 3,500-strong "Quebec Army," the first of the three forces to reach Montreal. When the other two armies arrived within the week from other directions, a surrounded Vaudreuil had little choice but to surrender.

On 8 September 1760 New France capitulated and Canada came under the British Crown. Led by massed bands, including the pipers of three Highland regiments, British troops marched into Montreal through the Récollets Gate (which stood where Notre Dame Street meets McGill Street today) and took possession of the town. Thompson became annoyed as did many of his ilk when he was confined to a camp outside Montreal, forbidden to enter the town to celebrate the victory. Amherst's memories of the drunken soldiery in Boston after the Louisbourg campaign guided his actions in ensuring rum rations were curtailed.

James, however, got a chance to visit the camp of the 42nd Foot, the Royal Highland Regiment. Early in October, the troops that were not assigned to the garrison of Montreal were marched off in various directions to occupy towns and forts across the former French colony, or boarded ships that would take them down-river to Quebec, Louisbourg, Halifax, New York or home. The Fraser Highlander contingent rejoined their regiment at Quebec, where they found several of the companies billeted in various towns and villages on both sides of the St. Lawrence River while five companies, including the grenadiers, served in the city garrison. Here the Frasers would remain until the end of the war.

During this period martial law prevailed in the conquered New France. General Murray was appointed military governor and military courts administered justice. According to some family accounts, Thompson had distinguished himself at the battle of Sillery, probably at the head of his grenadier company, and as a reward General Murray had offered him important positions within the province:

L'Hôpital général de Québec, 1775. The hospital was founded in 1692, and hundreds of French and British soldiers were treated here following the battles on the Plains of Abraham and at Sillery. General Montcalm, mortally wounded on 13 September 1759, was originally buried in a shell hole in the Ursuline Convent. Years later and with considerable ceremony, his remains were transferred to the small cemetery attached to the hospital, the oldest war cemetery in Canada, the final resting place for over 1,000 soldiers, sailors and *miliciens* of the French commander's former army. L'Hôpital général now serves as a long-term home for the care of the elderly. (Editor's Collection)

> ... after the pressure of duty had somewhat subsided, General Murray, who personally knew his merits, made him an offer of the situations, either of Barrack-Master of Quebec or of Town-Major of Montreal; but he gave the preference to the nature of duties he had to perform in the Engineer Department.[54]

Thompson would later claim that he had been "attached to the Engineers Department by orders of General James Murray then commander of the forces."[55] Also in 1760, Murray had made arrangements for Thompson to acquire a then-

---

54. "The Late Mr. J. Thompson," *Star and Commercial Advertiser*, 8 September 1830. This obituary notice was the first public appearance of this story, with the information likely being fed to the editor from James Thompson Jr. In 1898, the LHSQ published an identical version in its *Transactions*, New Series, No. 22 (1898) under the subheading "Concerning the Journal of James Thompson: 1758–1830." This description of Thompson's early offers of employment was likely exaggerated by the family – the appointments of town major or barrack master were plum positions usually offered to a senior captain, not a sergeant.
55. JTC – Anecdote 38.

vacant house on St. Louis Street under the terms of a "special mortgage." Located in the prestigious Upper Town just across from Parlour Street (which leads into the Ursuline Convent), the house and lot were originally the property of Michel Balan *dit* Lacombe. In 1727, the property had been mortgaged to Jean-François Tisseran De Montcharvaux, then a junior cavalry officer with the Governor's Guard, for 1,200 French livres. When Lacombe died, the mortgage was inherited by his young widow, Magdelaine Lachance. As soon as Quebec had fallen to the British, Tisseran had fled to Louisiana leaving 700 livres remaining on his loan.

A few years later, when Quebec returned to some semblance of order, and with Thompson still occupying the house, Lacombe's widow demanded that Thompson pay the remaining sum on her mortgage with Tisseran (700 French livres was approximately equivalent to £30 sterling). Thompson refused to pay, claiming that he was the rightful owner of the property by virtue of his arrangement with General Murray. Thompson remained in the house, but by 1767 the matter would end up in court.[56]

By November 1761 Thompson was once again detached to the Engineers Department, working as a writing clerk for Spry, who then held the rank of captain lieutenant. That same month, Spry wrote to Amherst telling him that he had been forced to retain Thompson to perform much needed clerical duties:

> I have been under the necessity of paying a Serjeant one shilling and six pence per day as a Clerk to keep my diaries and Accounts in a State of safety to the Engineer. This I required to be paid out of the Contingencies of the Army, but the Governor refused me. I hope my ordering payment for the same will meet with your Honours approbation. I beg pardon for troubling your Honours with this long detail and rely on your great goodness to forgive him who is, with the most profound respect… Your most devoted & most humble Servant, W. Spry, Engineer & Capt.-Lieut.[57]

---

56. "Magdelaine Lachance vs. James Thompson," 26 October 1767, BAnQ, TP5, S1, SS1-1980-09-008/1 dossier No. 293. That General Murray would bother to make such an arrangement for a lowly sergeant, when hundreds of officers would be looking for accommodation, speaks volumes for the family claim that Thompson had distinguished himself in battle. Most of the officers were quartered in the Intendant's Palace in Lower Town, some distance from the troops (for obvious reasons, the troops were quartered in Upper Town, close to the fortifications). Quebec City's dramatic topography, augmented by its man-made fortifications, divided the city into two distinct natural subdivisions, called Upper and Lower Town. The principal public and religious buildings together with offices, retail shops and prestigious homes stood in Upper Town, while Lower Town, with its vast warehouses and wharves was the focal point for commerce and maritime activity. For obvious reasons, the town's political, military and religious elite preferred Upper Town, while Lower Town became the home of merchants, craftspeople and workers.
57. William Spry to Jeffery Amherst et all, Quebec, 23 November 1761, Northcliffe Collection, Townshend Papers, LAC, MG18-L7, R-931.

The Treaty of Paris, signed on 10 February 1763, officially ended the Seven Years' War and France surrendered all claims to New France. It was a period of friction and adjustment for the French Canadians and the British. British merchants would soon be flocking to what was now called the British province of Quebec. General James Murray was appointed the first governor of the province (Captain General and Governor in Chief of the Province of Quebec) and he would govern Quebec almost as a Crown colony. Until a civil government was established on 15 October 1764 and the Ordinance Establishing Civil Courts was proclaimed, justice in the new province was administered by military courts.

Thompson got a taste of the new military courts when he was sued for repairs to his house on St. Louis Street. On 2 March 1763 a military court ordered Thompson to pay 849 shillings, 6 pence. He was also ordered to pay rent amounting to 400 livres per year.[58] Later that year, orders were received from London to disband Fraser's Highlanders. The officer supervising the reduction in accordance with the King's orders was none other than James Murray, Governor of the Province of Quebec, a fellow Scotsman who took more than a passing interest in the regiment's disbandment.

Some of the officers chose to remain in the colony (including Captain JOHN NAIRNE, and Lieutenants MALCOLM FRASER and ALEXANDER FRASER, who agreed to manage seigneuries which Murray had purchased from *Canadien* owners at bargain prices). One hundred and seventy sergeants, corporals, drummers and rank and file of the 78th also opted to take their discharge in America,[59] and of these eighty went south to New York to settle in the Mohawk Valley. Those who remained in Quebec "would act as tacksmen on Murray's seigneuries and served under their former company officers" while others "were interested in acquiring their own farms or were already engaged as tradesmen."[60]

It was inevitable that romances between the disbanded Highlanders and French-Canadian women developed:

> However, these conquering heroes faced a more formidable opponent in the form of the local priest, and his bishop, who were unwilling to solemnise marriages involving a Protestant groom. In Quebec in the 1760s and 1770s, many of

---

58. "Jean Guérault vs. James Thompson," Register, Military Court of Quebec (Conseil militaire de Québec), BAnQ, TL9, P5046, No. 5 (23 February 1764–4 August 1764), f. 13. The reasons for the repairs are not known.
59. "An account of His Majesty's Royal Bounty of Fourteen days Subsistence, also the sword money paid to the following men of the 78th Regiment Discharged in America," LAC, RG4-C2, vol 1, 1763 Letter-book, Microfilm C-10462.
60. Ian Macpherson McCulloch, *Sons of the Mountains: The Highland Regiments in the French and Indian War, 1757–1767* (hereafter McCulloch, *SOTM*), I (Purple Mountain Press, 2006), 308.

the Scottish soldiers and their Roman Catholic brides lived without benefit of clergy, although their children were baptized, albeit in many cases the entry by the local priest noted that the child was illegitimate. Also, there were very few Protestant clergy in the country, and the women and their families would probably have been very unhappy about marrying in a Protestant church.[61]

Any officer or soldier who opted to remain in Canada was rewarded by subsistence pay[62] and a grant of land, the extent of which depended on rank and length of service.[63] Some who did not wish to accept this offer were shipped back to Scotland for discharge in Glasgow. Others were drafted into regiments remaining in North America, to bring them up to proper strength.[64]

Thompson was one of those who took his discharge in Quebec. On the strength of his experience, Thompson landed a permanent civilian position as clerk of works with the Engineers Department, working first under Spry and later (1762) under JOHN MARR.[65] At this time, the offices of the Engineers Department were located in the Bishop's Palace, the former Episcopal Palace.[66]

It is believed that Thompson married shortly after the war, likely to a *Canadienne* as there would have been few British women in the garrison at that time. This is possibly the reason why General Murray allegedly gave him permission to occupy the house on St. Louis Street. Thompson is strangely silent about his first wife, to the point where he does not mention her name (or the name of the six children from this first union) in any of his diaries or journals. As a result,

---

61. Marie Fraser, "Conquering Canada on the plains of Germany," *Clan Fraser Society of Canada*, <http://www.clanfraser.ca/78th.htm> (accessed 8 August 2009). Today, descendants of these Highlanders may still be found on the banks of the St. Lawrence and particularly in the Fraserville or Rivière-du-Loup area, many of whom now speak only French.
62. Subsistence pay was a one-time payment normally awarded to discharged soldiers to "bring them home." A typical payment would be fourteen days subsistence, in other words, sufficient cash to carry them over a fourteen-day journey back to their home county.
63. The official statement read: "Grants are to be made only to such officers as have served in North America during the late war, and to such private soldiers only as have been or shall be disbanded in America, and are actually residing there." NA, Calendar of Home Office Papers, 1760–1765, vol 1 (London, 1878), 304.
64. Murray had reported to Amherst on 6 September 1763 that "the 15th, 27th and 2nd Battalion, Royal American Regiment were completed to the present establishment by drafts from the 47th and 78th Regiments."
65. Thompson would eventually work under six commanding engineers: William Spry, John Marr, William Twiss, Gother Mann, Ralph Henry Bruyères and Elias Walker Durnford.
66. The Bishop's Palace, built 1693–95, was situated at the top of Mountain Street (côte de la Montagne) and overlooked Lower Town. It suffered heavy damage during the 1759 bombardment and when rebuilt, sections were taken over by the British. In 1777 portions of the building were used to house the Legislative Council.

she is known to us only through his occasional references to the state of her health and to her burial location.[67]

Petitions for land grants to those soldiers discharged in Quebec started to show up in 1765. On 15 March, Thompson and eleven other discharged sergeants (ten from the 78th and two from the 2nd Battalion, Royal Americans), signed a joint application to Governor Murray requesting land grants "in or about the Bays of Gaspey or Chaleurs."[68] Thompson would make another land application some years later, this time with a French-Canadian, who was also a Captain of Militia (MICHEL "JOSÉ" BLAIS). He also helped other former soldiers petition for the land that was due to them, and his neat copperplate script appears on two submissions dated 19 May and 31 May 1765, also requesting lands near the bays of Gaspé and Chaleur.

In 1766, following a dispute with Quebec's British merchants over how the province would be governed, Governor Murray[69] was recalled to London. While he eventually cleared his name, he was replaced by GUY CARLETON, Wolfe's quartermaster general during the Quebec campaign. Meanwhile, Mrs. Lacombe had taken Thompson to court over his continued occupancy of her former house on St. Louis Street. In October 1767 a tribunal ruled in favour of the widow, which Thompson appealed. Under the terms of the "special mortgage" which he had obtained from General Murray, plus the fact that he had lived in the house for seven years, Thompson claimed that he was "master and owner" of the property. The court demanded that he provide adequate proof of ownership, and when he could not produce the necessary documentation, he was ordered to pay 700 livres to the widow, with interest from the day he first took occupancy.

The appeals court granted him "preferred occupancy" status with one year to "comply with the said award." On the other hand, Mrs. Lacombe was ordered to "give good and sufficient security in case the defendant was able to prove the mortgage in question to have been paid & that she may be obliged to give up the mortgage to the defendant."[70] An unhappy Thompson was also ordered to

---

67. In July 1867 James Thompson Jr. wrote the following in his journal: "The mother and six children of the first marriage [of his father], all died within a short space of each other." James Thompson Jr. Fonds, BAnQ, P254, 1972-00-085/12.
68. McCulloch, *SOTM*, I, 309. The list of names includes many of the soldiers who would feature in Thompson's anecdotes. No evidence has been found to show that this application was ever approved.
69. Murray was sympathetic to the French-Canadians, favouring them over British merchants who had come to settle in Quebec. The merchants had demanded not only an elected assembly but the introduction of English civil law, and when these demands were not met, they forced his recall (although he remained governor in name until 1768).
70. "Widow Lacombe vs. James Thompson," Register of the Court of Common Pleas of the District of Quebec (Judgements), 29 January 1765 to 1 August 1768, BAnQ, TP5, S1, SS11, D1, folio 288.

pay all court costs, including the provost marshal's fees and expenses. This was a substantial debt for a man of his limited means, but the alternative was to vacate the property and find other living accommodations. It would be difficult for Thompson, a civilian clerk, to stay in Upper Town, where prime properties were hard to come by.[71]

Over the period March 1769 to July 1770 Thompson was being paid "only sporadically and it had been necessary to stop projects after the commander-in-chief refused to approve a pay-roll signed by Thompson,"[72] so times must have been hard for Thompson and his growing family. Apparently, when he was on the payroll, he was paid four shillings "army currency" per day.[73]

In 1772 Captain Marr returned to Scotland on extended leave and Governor Carleton (stationed in New York) ordered Lieutenant Colonel VALENTINE JONES of the 52nd Regiment[74] to appoint an infantry or artillery officer to take over as head of military engineering services in Quebec, the normal practice when an engineer was not available. However, Colonel Jones was reluctant to appoint an officer from the garrison as he considered that such an officer would not be "acquainted with the forms of office, the framing of estimates, and the nature of Works and materials."[75]

As the position was of a temporary nature, and only until an engineering officer was posted to Quebec, Colonel Jones offered it to Thompson, presumably after clearing it with Carleton. Effective 25 October 1772, Thompson was appointed to the position and given the impressive title of overseer of works. More importantly, he was paid an extra two shillings and sixpence per day, a

---

71. In 1760, by right of conquest, the British appropriated 141 acres in Quebec: 127 in Upper Town, and 14 in Lower Town. Of the 127 acres in Upper Town, 67½ represented the existing defensive works (the western ramparts and their outworks alone covered 60 acres!), while 59¾ were reserved for future works (the Citadel, the Engineers Yard, the Esplanade, etc.).
72. Christian Rioux, "James Thompson." *DCB*, <http://www.biographi.ca/index-e.html> (accessed 9 August 2009).
73. During the Seven Years' War the British army had difficulty paying the troops which were stationed in different parts of North America, with each colony adopting a different currency system. In 1757 the treasury directed that local currency systems should be ignored and that all troops in North America should be paid in coins valued at the same rate. The basic coin was to be the Spanish dollar rated at four shillings and eight pence sterling (4s. 8d). In dealing with civilians in North America, the army continued to use local currency, usually Halifax currency, in which the dollar was rated at 5 shillings; £107.14 Halifax was equal to £100 army sterling. A.B. McCullough, *Money and Exchange in Canada to 1900* (Dundurn Press, 1999).
74. At this time the 52nd Regiment was in garrison in Quebec and its commander, Lieutenant Colonel Valentine Jones, was also commander of the forces in Canada.
75. JTC – Anecdote 38.

substantial increase to his salary.[76] Thompson "supervised repairs to military and government buildings and fortifications, made up payrolls, prepared estimates, bought construction materials, and negotiated contracts."[77] As the Engineers Department at Quebec was the only one for the whole colony, he would often superintend projects throughout the province. By this time, the offices of the Engineers Department had moved to Artillery Park, near the Palace Gate.[78]

Thompson carried out the duties of the *de facto* head of engineering services at Quebec for three and a half years "without any assistance of clerks or others," although he did receive the "approbation of the commander-in-chief" for his "economy in carrying on the necessary works and repairs throughout the Province."[79]

About 1773 a census was taken of the English population remaining in Quebec City:[80]

> *St. Louis Street*
> James Thompson, age 48
> Wife
> John McLane, boarder, age 40
> One woman servant

---

76. Thompson's base salary was four shillings; added to this was two shillings and six pence "extra pay" making his daily remuneration six shillings and six pence Army currency. He also received an additional annual payment of £20 for lodging, and he was entitled to an annual allotment of firewood and candles. At some later date, he lost most of his "extra pay" as in 1779, he petitioned the Duke of Kent for an increase in his salary, stating that his pay was four shillings and eight pence army currency. Prior to decimalization in the 1970s the pound (£) was divided into 20 shillings and each shilling into 12 pence, making 240 pence to the pound.
77. Rioux, "James Thompson," *DCB*.
78. Artillery Park, located next to the Dauphine Bastion, forms a crucial part of Quebec's fortifications, having been the main barracks and arsenal under the French regime. Consisting of the massive Dauphine Barracks, the Arsenal Foundry and the two-storey Artillery Barracks (built by the French over the period 1749–54 as the *Nouvelles Casernes* or "New Barracks"), the Park was taken over by the Royal Artillery in 1766, with offices and living spaces also provided to the Corps of Engineers.
79. JTC – Anecdote 38.
80. Census of the English population living in Quebec circa 1773 (*Recensement de la population anglais demeurant à Québec vers 1773*, Archives du Séminaire de Québec, Polygraphie 37, No. 1.) With war between Britain and the American colonists looming, this census was taken to determine the "Anglo" population of Quebec who could bear arms. While Thompson's age is shown as forty-eight, this is likely a transcription error and should be forty (in the 19th century, the number 8 was written as a 0 with a horizontal line through the centre, leading to some confusion between 0s and 8s) Thompson's boarder, John McLane, was a former sergeant from the 78th Foot (Fraser's Highlanders) and a fellow Freemason..

As previously discussed, it is believed that Thompson and his wife had six children, yet no children appear in this census. This suggests that the children had all died sometime before 1773, perhaps from a contagious disease such as smallpox. Also, Thompson had retained the services of a resident housekeeper.[81]

Later that year, Thompson was sent to the town of Three Rivers (Trois-Rivières) to oversee the erection of a large magazine and storehouse to be used by German troops quartered in that area. The work, which included the excavation of a cellar at one end, cost £150 to erect, all performed by local workers. Thompson was proud of his accomplishment as he later recorded that "no person unacquainted with the prices of work and materials, and the peculiar customs of the country, could have completed buildings of the same dimensions for double the sum."[82]

In 1775 momentous events were happening south of the border. Following skirmishes with the British army at Lexington and Concord in Massachusetts, a rebel army had been formed with George Washington as its commander. Rebel Brigadier Generals BENEDICT ARNOLD and RICHARD MONTGOMERY were ordered to march against Quebec. Thompson was still acting as the *de facto* head of engineering services and, with Quebec threatened, Governor Carleton[83] recalled him from Three Rivers to put Quebec's fortifications "in a state of defence at a time when there was not a single article of material in store...."[84]

As time was of the essence, Thompson's defensive arrangements could only be hastily built works, such as temporary barricades and palisades,[85] but he was ordered to purchase all required materials and "to prosecute the work with the greatest dispatch."[86] Thompson, ever the penurious Scotsman, managed to purchase all of the timber he needed for less than a thousand pounds, considerably less than the original asking price – for Thompson, saving a few pounds was essential, even in a national emergency!

Thompson began work at Palace Gate with only fourteen Canadian car-

---

81. The fact that Thompson retained a servant is confirmed by two entries in his journal: 2 July 1785, when he wrote that hurricane force winds had broken many windows in Quebec, including some in his own lodging, and his "wife, child and servant was much frightened"; and 28 January 1786, when he wrote "my servant girl departed this life."
82. JTC – Anecdote 38.
83. Guy Carleton served two terms as governor. His first term covered 1768–78 (as governor of the Province of Quebec), while his second term covered 1786–96 (first as governor of the Province of Quebec, then as governor general of Canada).
84. JTC – Anecdote 38. At this time, Thompson was still the effective head of military engineering services at Quebec. He would step down only when Captain Marr returned.
85. A palisade is a fence of closely-set, pointed wooden stakes.
86. JTC – Anecdote 38.

penters but was quickly reinforced with two artificer companies,[87] the first from Halifax and the second from Newfoundland. He set the men to work palisading the open ground on Cape Diamond; framing and erecting a large blockhouse on the outside of the St. Louis Gate; building a blockhouse under the Cape Diamond Bastion; laying platforms; repairing the embrasures; and erecting barricades at the extremities of Lower Town. Finally, he blocked the windows and provided musketry loopholes in all the houses facing the riverside, "in case the river should freeze across."[88]

Since the Americans arrived at Quebec late in the year, they could not organize a conventional siege but set up a blockade in an attempt to cut communications between Quebec's Upper Town and the surrounding countryside. On 3 November, Brigadier General Benedict Arnold, in command of over 700 American troops, emerged from the woods at the settlements along the Chaudière River. Crossing the St. Lawrence on the night of 14 November, Arnold had his men parade in front of the St. Louis Gate, where he saluted the town with three cheers, "fully expecting that the gates would be opened for their reception."[89] At this time, Thompson was waiting on the Cape Diamond[90] Bastion, where he "levelled and fired a 24-pounder at them which had the effect of making them disperse hastily."[91] Arnold quickly retreated to Pointe-aux-Trembles,[92] just west of the city, and continued the blockade.

On 1 December 1775 the British garrison could only muster 1,800 men to defend Quebec, including Thompson and his 120 artificers. In addition to his work on Quebec's defences, which required him to ride to and from the various stations on horseback, Thompson and his artificers performed nightly picquet duties. "This we continued to do during the blockade, nor have I laid down on a bed during all that time," recorded Thompson many years later.[93] At forty-two years of age, this strenuous workload would have future health repercussions, such as a persistent cough and bouts of rheumatism. After completing the defensive works, Thompson and his men served as soldiers, forming part of Quebec's reserves under the command of Major John Nairne, a former officer with Fra-

---

87. Artificers, also known as soldier-artificers, were artisans, tradesmen or labourers raised from the local pool of suitably qualified civilians and used for military engineering tasks. They were officered by the Corps of Engineers.
88. JTC – Anecdote 38.
89. *Ibid.*
90. In French, Cap Diamant. The Cape Diamond promontory is the highest point in the headland (333 feet) and is today crowned by the Citadel. The cape was named by Samuel de Champlain in 1608, who found quartz crystals resembling diamonds.
91. JTC – Anecdote 38.
92. Today the village of Neuville.
93. JTC – Anecdote 38.

ser's Highlanders. The blockade continued during the month of December with American troops established in every house near the walls, especially in the St. Roch suburb near the Intendant's Palace.

During this time, Thompson had devised an innovative scheme to illuminate the open ground in front of the ramparts on dark nights. This involved attaching lanterns to long poles extended beyond the bastion salient points. According to Thompson, "by means of these lights, even a dog could be distinguished if in the great-ditch, in the darkest night."[94]

By now Arnold's forces had been reinforced by additional troops under Brigadier General Richard Montgomery. Montgomery, in overall command, decided to storm the city rather than continue the blockade. During a blinding snowstorm on the morning of 31 December 1775, Montgomery led his troops through a narrow defile in Lower Town known as Près-de-Ville. Thompson had placed a barrier across this defile, with a cannon placed on the second floor of an adjacent building. As soon as the Americans came within range the cannon, loaded with canister shot, was discharged at point-blank range. Montgomery and a few of his men, including two officers and a sergeant, were instantly killed. The surprise of a cannon discharge in the dead of night, coupled with the loss of their commanding officer, took the heart out of the attackers and they beat a swift retreat, leaving their dead behind. Meanwhile, another attack by Arnold was also repulsed, and essentially the battle for Quebec was over, although the blockade would not be effectively lifted until the Royal Navy arrived on 6 May 1776 with much-needed reinforcements.

As soon as things quieted down, Governor Carleton sent Thompson out with a search party to bring in the dead for decent burial and to see if any of the wounded had been overlooked. The search party came across a frozen hand protruding vertically from the knee-deep snow. The hand belonged to General Montgomery's frozen corpse, a gruesome sight that would stick in Thompson's memory for the rest of his life. The general's sword was found near by and was quickly snatched up by a drummer boy. As the senior officer present, Thompson later claimed the sword, although he gave the lad seven shillings and sixpence "by way of prize money."[95]

Thompson left an interesting account of how, under his superintendence, Montgomery's body was identified by Mrs. Miles Prentice, who, with her husband MILES PRENTICE, then kept Free Masons' Hall,[96] a frequent stop by Mont-

---

94. *Ibid*. Thompson uses the term "lanthorn" in his memoirs. Later, the lanterns were augmented with barrels of tar that were then ignited.
95. JTC – Anecdote 29. The sword remained in the family long after Thompson's death in 1830.
96. The hall was located on the old site of the famous Chien d'Or (or Golden Dog) to which

The Death of General Montgomery at Quebec. John Trumbull's historical painting of the death of Brigadier General Richard Montgomery leaves much to be desired. Montgomery is shown stuck in a pose similar to that Michelangelo's *La Pietà* (1499), and Trumbull may have based this work on Jacques-Louis David's *The Oath of the Horatti* (1785) where three classical figures raise their arms to swear an oath of vengeance. In any event, like Benjamin West's *The Death of General Wolfe*, Montgomery's senior officers assuredly did not gather round him in a picturesque group as depicted here. Print of an engraving by C.W. Ketterlinus after a 1786 painting by John Trumbull. (LOC LC-USZ62-76464)

gomery during his earlier business visits to Quebec. With Montgomery positively identified, Carleton ordered Thompson to bury the general with reasonable ceremony. Having a suitable coffin built by a local carpenter, Thompson made arrangements to bury General Montgomery, a Protestant, inside the gorge of the St. Louis Bastion and close to the grave of his first wife, this area still being used as a Protestant cemetery.[97] Burial in an obscure cemetery by torchlight in

---

so much of Quebec's romantic history is attached. Sometime after 1771, the property was acquired by Miles Prentice, who converted it to a hotel and boarding house known as Free Mason's Hall. The hotel was patronized by Quebec's leading citizens and Freemasons, as well as the British officers of the garrison (including Captain Richard Montgomery of the 17th Regiment, the same Richard Montgomery who was killed in action at Près-de-Ville in 1775). When Prentice died in 1787, his wife continued to operate the hotel for some years. Eventually the Freemasons purchased the property.
97. The Protestant cemetery on St. John Street had been in use since 1772. However, it

the dead of night, with no public signs of respect, and without the honours of war, was a sad and unusual end for the former British officer turned American patriot. It suggests a degree of unstated animosity between Brigadier General Montgomery and Governor Carleton. As historian Paul Reynolds has observed, "here at Québec, lay a former officer of the British Army ... at the time of his death ... a rebel fighting his former comrades. To Carleton, Montgomery must have seemed a most reprehensible turncoat."[98]

Thompson would later claim that Montgomery's sword was "silver-mounted, but altogether but a poor-looking thing," but a magnet for "receiving the visits of a great number of American ladies and gentlemen, who put so many questions to me, that I am heartily tired of answering them, now that old-age has got the better of me."[99]

In 1879 author Thomas Jones published an interesting, but fanciful, account that had apparently been related to him by Thompson's son, John Gawler.[100] While visiting Quebec in the summer of 1866, Jones was told that James Thompson had been unable to sleep during the evening of 31 December 1775, this from "a presentiment of impending danger." According to John Gawler, his father had awoken before daybreak and thought it was necessary to examine the outworks on the St. Charles side of the city. Snow covered the ground, and it was snowing slightly at the time.

As daylight was starting to break, Thompson noticed some indistinct white objects at a distance which seemed to be moving. He immediately reported his observations to General Carleton, and orders were sent throughout the city to be on the alert. According to the story, the result was that when Montgomery made his attack, "he found the British prepared, and was killed at the first fire." Later, James Thompson had learned that the American troops had put white shirts over their clothes, so as to "destroy the contrast with the snow on the ground, and prevent their being discovered too soon." As Jones concluded, "thus the presentiment of James Thompson was really the cause of Montgomery's defeat and death."[101]

---

was situated "outside" the fortification walls and could not be used to bury General Montgomery while Quebec was blockaded by the Americans. The gorge was the interior side of a bastion: it formed the work's entranceway. In Anecdote 29, Thompson tells us that he buried his first wife "within, and near the surrounding wall of the powder magazine, in the gorge of the St. Louis Bastion."

98. Paul R. Reynolds, *Guy Carleton, a Biography* (New York, 1980).
99. JTC – Anecdote 17.
100. Thomas Jones, *A History of New York During the Revolutionary War and of Leading Events in the other Colonies at that Period*, vol 1 (New York, 1879), 729.
101. Another former Fraser Highlander claimed to be the first to observe the American attack on 31 December 1775, Lieutenant Malcolm Fraser. In his 31 March 1791 memorial to Guy Carleton, Fraser (then a captain with the 84th Foot, Royal Highland Emigrants) stated

During the American attack, Thompson had observed a daring feat of bravery by FRANÇOIS DAMBOURGÈS, then serving with the Royal Highland Emigrants.[102] In 1822 an effort was made to obtain a pension for his surviving daughters and Thompson, an eyewitness, was asked to write an account of his bravery:

> Quebec, 17 April 1822 – Sir, Agreeable to your request, I am to relate to you what I recollect of the late Lieutenant Dambourgès of the late 84th Regiment, and I can truly say, that I have known him to be a vigilant, active and brave officer on all occasions, particularly during the American blockade of Quebec in the winter of 1775; that the enemy made an attack on the Lower Town on the morning of 31st December of that year when Lieutenant Dambourgès, with the late Lieutenant Colonel Nairn, did, by the means of a ladder, enter through a window of a house in Sault-au-Matelot, then occupied by the enemy, and by this bold attempt the enemy abandoned the house, and by this Colonel Nairn's party which followed him and Dambourgès through the same window and by another party arriving nearly at the same time at the north end of the street, that part of the enemy were made prisoners. I have the honor, &c., Jas. Thompson.[103]

With the blockade winding down and arrival of reinforcements, Thompson found himself "quite worn down with fatigue and anxiety." He remained in his bed in a "debilitated state" for fourteen days, blaming it all on his exertions over the previous six months, adding that his "ultimate recovery was extremely tedious."[104]

Sometime after May 1777 Thompson's first wife died.[105] As it appears that his

---

"on going his rounds as Captain of the main guard ... had the good fortune to be the first ... who discovered by some signals that the enemy intended an attack and having immediately reported to your Lordship, you was pleased to order the alarm to be given and thus the Garrison had time to receive them." LAC, RG8 "C" Series, Microfilm C-2610.

102. Raised in 1775 as a two battalion regiment on the provincial establishment by Lieutenant Colonel Allan Maclean, the 1st Battalion formed part of Quebec's garrison during the blockade of 1775–76. The regiment was placed on the British regular establishment as the 84th Regiment of Foot (Royal Highland Emigrants) in 1779. It was disbanded in June 1784.

103. James Thompson to Colonel John Hale, Quebec, 17 April 1822, LAC, RG8 "C" Series, Microfilm C-2781. See also: Anonymous, *Le Colonel Dambourgès – étude historique canadienne* (Quebec, 1866), 30.

104. JTC – Anecdote 38.

105. JTC. In his journal entry on 23 September 1782 Thompson tells us that his first wife died as a result of a breast infection following the birth of a child. In Anecdote 29, Thompson tells us that he buried General Richard Montgomery "just along side of that of my first Wife." This wording has led many historians to believe that his first wife had predeceased Montgomery, i.e. she died sometime before the end of 1775. However, a recently discovered letter from Thompson to John Gawler, proves that she was still alive (but quite ill from the effects of a breast infection) as late as 21 May 1777 (James Thompson to John Gawler, Quebec, 21 May 1777, James Thompson Jr. Fonds, BAnQ, P254-1972-00-087). Therefore, the editors believe that Thompson's first wife likely died in the latter half of 1777. As Thompson's second wife, Fanny Cooper, suffered from a

children had all predeceased her, Thompson was now alone. It must have been a devastating blow, but again he is strangely silent on his loss. We are only told that he buried her (no mention of any children) in the gorge of the St. Louis Bastion. At this time, a section of the gorge was still being used as a special Protestant cemetery.[106]

In late 1777 Lieutenant WILLIAM TWISS,[107] a veteran of Major General John Burgoyne's army that had surrendered to the Americans at Saratoga in October 1777, was exchanged and joined the Engineers Department at Quebec, working under Captain Marr. FREDERICK HALDIMAND, who replaced Guy Carleton as Governor General of the Province of Quebec in June 1778, had a high opinion of Twiss, and things began to sour for the aged and infirm John Marr.

Although Marr was the commanding engineer at Quebec, most command decisions were now made by Twiss, causing Marr to complain to Haldimand that reports were not made to him as commanding engineer and that he was being treated "as a cypher." Furthermore, Marr pointed out to Haldimand that he believed that an injustice was done to him "by the appointment of a junior engineer to the command of the Engineers"[108] and requested permission to return to England "to prevent the effects of such treatment."[109] When Marr left in 1781, the newly promoted Captain Lieutenant Twiss assumed the duties of commanding engineer in Canada.

In 1780 Thompson's eye for detail and memories of General Wolfe were called into service for the ornamentation of a niche above a two-storey building's entrance at the corner of St. John and Palace Streets (rue St-Jean and rue des

---

similar condition, the root cause of their affliction will be covered in more detail later in this monograph.

106. P.-G. Roy, *Les Cimetières de Québec* (Lévis, 1941), 253–4. Starting in 1767, Quebec's small Protestant population made use of the gorge of the St. Louis Bastion (near the St. Louis Gate) for their burials. The first burials were recorded by the garrison's chaplain, Rev. John Brooke, but when he returned to England he took the register of births, marriages and burials with him. He was replaced by David-François de Montmollin in the spring of 1768, but he was apparently negligent is his record-keeping duties as the surviving register book only lists 100 burials in spite of the fact that almost all of the Protestants who died in Quebec from 1767 to 1772 were buried in this cemetery. Known to the English as the St. Louis Gate Cemetery, it remained Quebec's only Protestant cemetery until the cemetery on St. John Street opened in 1772. After 1772, burials at the St. Louis Gate Cemetery were rare, however, one burial did occur as late as 8 November 1791. Burying his wife in a Protestant cemetery suggests two possibilities: one, she was Protestant (therefore likely of British origin); or two, she was an excommunicated Roman Catholic (perhaps of French or French-Canadian origin) and thus denied burial in a Catholic cemetery.

107. Twiss was chief engineer in Canada from 1778 to 1783.

108. Captain John Marr to General Frederick Haldimand, Quebec, 4 August 1778, LAC, Sessional Papers (No. 5A), 52 Victoria, A. 1889, page 611.

109. *Ibid.*, 31 July 1778.

Pauvres, today known as côte du Palais). Sometime previously, its pious owner had filled the niche with a statue of St. John the Baptist. After the surrender, the owner, fearing the British "barbarians" might lack proper respect for the saint's effigy, had it relocated to the General Hospital.

For many years, the house with the unoccupied niche was simply an inconspicuous building on St. John Street. Then on 20 April 1780 the property was bought by George Hipps, a butcher, who had decided to use the niche to some higher purpose. Being a loyal Britisher, Hipps could not think of anyone more worthy of honour than James Wolfe, the famous general under whom he had once served. The previous year, Hipps had hired Thomas-Hyacinthe and Ives Chaulette, two brothers who were local sculptors, to execute a large wooden statue of Wolfe. Knowing that Thompson and Wolfe were more than passing acquaintances, he asked Thompson to give the sculptors a good description of Wolfe's features.[110] Thompson drew some sketches and often visited the sculptors' workshop while the statue was being carved, but the result was not very satisfactory. With his usual eye for the absurd, Thompson thought "they made but a poor job of it after all, for the front-face is no likeness at all, and the profile is all that they could hit upon.... I say we made but a poor General Wolfe of it...."[111] The corner of Palace and St. John streets was subsequently known as Wolfe's Corner.[112]

Unfortunately, Hipps would not enjoy his new statue for long, as he died in 1781. However, it would appear that the sculptors had sources for Wolfe's appearance other than Thompson's memory. In 1846 the old Hipps house was purchased by Isaac Dorion, a builder who intended to erect a new building on the lot. During demolition, Dorion found a hand-coloured mezzotint (14.3 × 10

---

110. This shows that Thompson's stories about Wolfe and Fraser's Highlanders were starting to become popular in Quebec.
111. JTC – Anecdote 8. The statue has been in the collection of LHSQ since 1899.
112. In 1838, Wolfe's statue, then presenting a rather woebegone appearance from the effects of Quebec's weather, was "borrowed" by visiting midshipmen from HMS *Inconstant*, thinking that old "General Wolfe" would be improved by a sea voyage to warmer climes. The frigate eventually made its way to Portsmouth, having first visited Halifax and Bermuda. The following year, having thought better of their prank, the midshipmen returned the statue complete with a new coat of paint and varnish. By 1898, after years of more exposure to the elements, it was necessary to remove the statue from its niche. By this time, "Wolfe's Corner" had been purchased by the Bell Telephone Company of Canada. The company's president, C.F. Sise, cognizant of the statue's history, had old "General Wolfe" properly preserved and repainted. In December 1898 he presented it to LHSQ for safe keeping, with the sole condition that it should be placed where it might be seen by visitors, but not exposed to the weather. It now rests in the peaceful environment of the society's library. Another wood sculpture of General Wolfe was crafted and installed in place of the original. It is not known when this facsimile was removed or its current whereabouts, but it remained at "Wolfe's Corner" until at least 1904.

Wolfe's Corner, Quebec, 1830. This detail of Image 5 on page 106 (see "A Colour Album") shows the wood statue of "General Wolfe" proudly standing in the corner niche at "Wolfe's Corner," the name given to the junction of Palace and St. John streets. In 1898, after years of exposure to the elements, the statue was restored and presented to the Literary and Historical Society of Quebec with the sole condition that it should be placed where it might be seen by visitors, but not exposed to the weather. "General Wolfe" now rests in the peaceful environment of the society's library. Watercolour by James Pattison Cockburn. (Royal Ontario Museum 951x205.17)

inches) of the full-length Wolfe by the Irish engraver Richard Houston which corresponded exactly to the coloured statue. It is reasonable to presume that the mezzotint was obtained by George Hipps from England to serve as a model for his wood statue.[113]

In 1779, acting on direct orders from London, Haldimand directed Twiss to begin construction of a temporary citadel in Quebec, a massive undertaking that would take many years to complete.[114] The Engineers Department in Quebec, forced to expand, took up new quarters in the Bishop's Palace. In late 1779 or early 1780 Thompson was given an apartment in the Palace; by this time, he was supervising all of the artificers and labourers employed by the Engineers Department.

Up until this time, most of the craftsmen and day-labourers who worked on the fortifications had been supplied by the troops then in garrison in Quebec. The new citadel, however, would require additional manpower, and in Twiss's estimation would take twelve to fifteen years, taking into account Quebec's long winters and, equally important, the "attitude of the local labour force."[115] This attitude was bypassed by hiring skilled workers from other parts of the colony, but the preference was still to use military labour as much as possible. As a result, soldiers from two German mercenary regiments stationed nearby were pressed into work. When work on the temporary citadel began in October 1779, the Germans represented 77 per cent of the total work force.

While this work kept the overseer of works very busy, Thompson was also required to perform special duties across the province. For example, in November 1779 he was ordered to Berthier in St. Thomas parish to oversee the building of storehouses large enough to contain nine months of provisions for German mercenary troops quartered in that area; and in 1780 he made plans and estimates to erect "three piles of barracks for the reception of Rebel Prisoners"[116]

---

113. P.-B. Casgrain, "The Monument to Wolfe on the Plains of Abraham, and the Old Statue at 'Wolfe's Corner,'" *Transactions, Royal Society of Canada*, Ser. II (1904), 213–22. Houston's mezzotint of Schaak's full-length General Wolfe had been executed in 1760.

114. A citadel is a fortress in or near a city. A well-designed citadel would provide a strong defensive position, but more importantly, it could be used as a final refuge for the garrison – an important consideration for the British at Quebec as they distrusted the local population until the day they left Quebec (1871). Marr had first recommended a citadel in 1760, and this recommendation had been repeated by commanding engineers during the second half of the 18th century. Land at Cape Diamond had been appropriated under Murray as early as 1763, although construction of a temporary citadel (e.g., built of earth and wood) was not started until 1779, and then only as a result of the American Revolutionary War. Construction of a permanent citadel was only started in May 1820 and it was finally completed in November 1831.

115. JTC.

116. *Ibid*.

on John Nairne's seigneury at La Malbaie. For the Malbaie project, Thompson used American prisoners who were carpenters or masons or had other construction talents. Thompson hired a schooner and made the trip from Quebec to La Malbaie. He remained there until the "mason work rose about a foot from the surface," at which time he returned to Quebec. On his return he learned that all the prisoners had escaped, stealing two bateaux from the harbour and crossing the river to Kamouraska. The next day he learned that local inhabitants had brought back all of the escaped prisoners, and as Thompson later recorded, "the men were generously rewarded."[117]

By about this time, Thompson was starting to realize that the work on Cape Diamond would be enormous, with the potential for many work-related problems, particularly from the new breed of assistant engineers soon to arrive. His apprehensions were expressed by the following entry in his journal:

> Having been employed in the Engineer's department from my coming into Canada … in June 1759 till the present time, and during that period of 20 years, had the good fortune of pleasing every Engineer under whom I served. I think it would go hard with me now to be brow-beat by such as may be employed as assistant engineers on these extensive works, from such circumstances I must confess I have my apprehensions.[118]

As a result, he decided to keep an "official" journal of his activities, as a precaution should he ever need to justify his conduct:

> I have therefore determined to take down some Memorandums, and occurrences relative to the works, by way of a Journal, with a view to refer to them, if unhappily I should be involved into any difficulty, when bare memory may not be sufficient to extricate me out of it, by which means, it is possible, I may have it in my power to clear myself even beyond contradiction.[119]

Thompson's fears about his looming responsibilities are understandable as the planned new defensive works went far beyond his previous experience and he would have to learn new skills "on the job." However, he trusted:

> … with a little practice and attention, I may get through with it, as I have formerly done, tho' not altogether with the same facility, having then youth on my side, which perhaps is now left too far behind to supply my present faculties with an equal share of assistance. Let that be as it may, I have the pleasing reflection yet before me, that I am still possessed of the same anxiety of doing my duty to the best in my power, and the same wish to please my superior offic-

---

117. *Ibid.* – Anecdote 38.
118. JTC. Undated but part of his introductory notes.
119. *Ibid*.

ers. This I thank God has always been an unalterable maxim with me in every station of life that Providence has placed me.[120]

In February 1780 Thompson paid a surprise visit to his old landlord from his campaigning days, Michel "José" Blais, who lived near St. Pierre (Saint-Pierre-de-la-Rivière-du-Sud). Thompson had first met Michel in 1760 when his grenadier company had been moved to St. Pierre, and Thompson had been billeted with his family. Michel was the eldest son of Pierre Blais, a well-to-do farmer who had died in 1733. Under the French regime, Michel had become a wealthy landowner and a captain of militia.[121] Michel was not home and the family did not recognize Thompson. However, as soon as Michel arrived, he joyfully welcomed Thompson back into his home, and the family members then clung

> about me as if they were ready to devour me, being eighteen years out of their sight, it is no wonder they did not know me, nor did I know any but the old lady and my landlord, those I left [as] children now at full growth, some of them married out and others then unborn....[122]

The Blais family, like some other *Canadien* families loyal to the British Crown, had been harshly treated by the American rebels, their property and lands plundered. Michel asked Thompson to help him petition the government to obtain some unoccupied waste lands adjacent to his property as compensation for his losses, and on 9 February 1779 the two friends made a joint application for a land grant in the Township of Armagh. However, the government kept this application, and likely many others, on a back burner for many years.

By March 1780 the expanded Engineers Department comprised the following:[123]

> Captain John Wade, Engineer
> Lieutenant J. Davis, Assistant Engineer
> James Thompson, Overseer of Works
> Edward Burford, Overseer of Works
> James Gill, Clerk
> Daniel Cameron, Conductor of Stores.

---

120. *Ibid.*
121. A *capitaine de milice* under the former French regime was an important man in the colony, particularly in the rural parishes. As the unpaid representative of the governor and intendant, he supervised the *corvée* (work on roads or bridges and the transportation of supplies), published edicts, administered minor justice and acted as a notary. The Canadian militia had been abolished at the end of November 1765 with the captains replaced by "bailiffs" in each parish. When the militia was restored in 1775, just before the American invasion, many of the former captains had their commissions reinstated, including Michel Blais.
122. JTC.
123. *Ibid.*

Twiss was in overall command but stationed at Halifax. Wade was the senior engineer at Quebec. An important change, one with serious implications for Thompson, was the addition of a second overseer of works, Edward Burford. Now, the artisans and labourers were divided between Thompson and Burford and it is not surprising that problems quickly developed. Things came to a head when Thompson needed to complete some labour distribution forms, and he asked the foreman in charge of carpenters (Mr. Bellamy) to assist him. Bellamy refused, telling Thompson that he "was accountable only to the master carpenter," Edward Burford. Incensed, Thompson was convinced that "Burford was determined to quarrel with me at all events."[124] Following protocol, Thompson escalated the matter to Captain Wade:

> 11 December 1779 – Met with Capt. Wade … to whom I represented the treatment I met with yesterday from Mr. Burford through Bellamy, and begged he would speak with Burford, that a stop may be put to such proceedings, lest attempts of the kind, tho' yet perhaps triffling [sic] may in a short time become serious, that in all my services I have done my duty quietly & without offence, but was not satisfied now that the master carpenter [Burford] should interfere with me in it.[125]

Wade cautioned Thompson that "Twiss & Burford was so much link'd together, that if I quarrelled with the one it will be doing it with both." Thompson then told Wade that "while he was but a stranger to Captain Twiss as yet," he had the opinion that Twiss would not "espouse a wrong cause, and that he knew his duty too well to suffer a breach of subordination."[126] Two days later, with no help evidently coming from Wade, Thompson fired off a letter to Twiss. Meanwhile, Thompson kept his distance from Burford and Bellamy, fearing "disagreeable altercations might happen," and patiently waited for Twiss to respond.

On 21 December 1779 Twiss wrote back to Thompson advising that he would make "such arrangements as appears to be necessary on the occasion."[127] Thompson had already formed a good opinion of Twiss and he was satisfied that the commanding engineer would "clear up to every one in the Department their respective duties, and put a final stop to the arrogance of the author of my complaint."[128] The following journal entry is of interest:

> 22 March 1780 – Hoped there should be no more rangling [sic] between me & Mr. Burford. He [Twiss] remarked at the same time, that Mr. Burford's temper was such as he himself could not put up with, but on account of his usefulness

---

124. *Ibid.*
125. *Ibid.*
126. *Ibid.*
127. *Ibid.*
128. *Ibid.*

must overlook his oddity, and wished I would not take notice of every triffle. That he spoke to him about what had happened, and that his apology was his ignorance of my connection with the Department.[129]

Twiss resolved the difficulties by issuing detailed instructions that clearly defined everyone's responsibilities.[130] Thompson and Burford were expressly ordered to obey Captain Wade and that "no stores of any kind to be purchased, and no artificers, labourers, or horses, etc., to be employed or discharged without his orders or approbation...." Each day at noon, both overseers were required to submit a written account of the number of fatigue men who would be required the following day.

Thompson was given the direction of all miners and labourers, while Burford would be in charge of all other artificers, "consequently the buildings and repairs of all magazines, storehouses, barracks, guard houses, sentry boxes, etc., will become his duty." As for the miners, Thompson was to ensure that all tools were "narrowly" inspected and that the men were provided with the right tools for their jobs and, under Wade's authority, to purchase all stores and materials that were needed for his projects. All receipts were to be "lodged in the office for inspection by Captain Wade."[131]

Thompson's orders specified that he must "pay particular attention that every branch of his business was carried out in the most expeditious manner" and that he be attentive that "every transport of stones and earth is done with the least work possible." When Thompson needed the assistance of carpenters or other artificers not under his authority, he was required to ask for assistance from Burford, "who must immediately comply with his demand." In turn, Thompson was required to give Burford "every necessary assistance to the public service...." Twiss added the following cautionary note at the end of his regulations:

> In carrying on Public works, Captain Twiss has always considered every degree of private jobbing as a species of dishonesty, and as a disgrace to every officer employed in the Department, and he is happy to think, that no work were every yet carried on where fewer abuses of his kind were committed. Indeed in our present situation, we should be doubly guilty if we permit it, and therefore we must all heartily join in promoting the Public Service; which never can be done effectually, unless we persevere rigidly in preventing so illegal a practice.[132]

Construction of the temporary citadel moved ahead slowly, primarily due to the lack of specialized manpower such as miners and quarrymen. After two

---

129. *Ibid.*
130. *Ibid.*, "Regulations by Captain Twiss Commanding Engineer in Canada for Carrying on the Fortifications at Quebec, during the year 1780...," journal entry, 22 March 1780.
131. *Ibid.*
132. *Ibid.*

and a half years of effort, Thompson reported that "not one piece of work [is] yet finished, every place overrun with cut stone and rubbish from the excavation ... a knowing eye only can make anything of the nature of the works but a mere confusion ..."[133]

> Thompson maintained that the Germans, working as miners on Cape Diamond, were slow, but when compared to Canadians, he had no grounds for complaint. He observed on 29 July 1780 that "their work is much preferable to any done in this country by the hands of a Canadian, besides they are constant and do not require much looking after, but they must have Profiles to work by."[134]

In spite of his heavy work load, squabbling with Burford and his many travels across the countryside, Thompson managed to find time for affairs of the heart. On 8 March 1780 he took an afternoon pleasure trip "up country" to Pointe-aux-Trembles with his friend Mrs. Miles Prentice and her pretty twenty-two-year-old niece, Fanny Cooper.[135] Fanny, recently arrived from Ireland, was assigned a seat in Thompson's cariole.[136] Thompson was quickly smitten – within a few months he would be referring to Fanny as his "great favourite" and his "lovely girl":

> 16 July 1780 – Sunday. Dined with Capt. Wade at his Country House, drank too much wine in so hot a season, and tho' I was not intoxicated with it felt it most disagreeably, returned home about 7 o'clock, called in at Mr. Prentice's to see Miss Fanny Cooper, a great favourite, and to mend the matter was obliged to drink more wine through the means of Lieut. Jonathan Prentice just arrived from Montreal....

> 21 November 1780 – Having received orders to go once more to Pointe aux Trembles, sat [sic] off at 10 o'clock, in this trip I contrived it so as to get Miss Fanny Cooper to favour me with her company, from whom I have contracted the greatest esteem for some time, and I find it daily growing upon me, tho' I have endeavoured to conceal it from her, and the world, till within a few days past I have found an opportunity of expressing to my lovely girl the passion I had for her & allowed her some time to consider of it, and thought this a favourable opportunity, Mrs. Prentice and her other relation were of the party, Miss Fanny being in my carriage, our conversation was confined to the object

---

133. JTC.
134. *Ibid.*
135. Frances "Fanny" Cooper was born on 25 December 1758 near Lake Killarney, county Kerry, Ireland. Fanny had come to Quebec on the invitation of her aunt, Mrs. Miles Prentice (née Cooper). Fanny's aunt on her father's side had married Miles Prentice, a sergeant in the 43rd Foot (Kennedy's). When the 43rd was sent to Canada at the start of the Seven Years' War, Prentice managed to have his wife accompany his regiment. The couple remained in Quebec at the end of the war.
136. A cariole was a small carriage drawn by a single horse.

of my view and wishes, and before we reached the end of our journey she so far completed my happiness as to promise her hand.

30 November 1780 – Dined in the Lower Town with a few of the sons of St. Andrew, which prevented my returning to the Cape for the rest of the day. Anxious to complete my happiness with Miss Fanny Cooper, made my intentions known to my best friend Mrs. Simpson, who did not seem pleased with my being connected with Mrs. Prentice, on account of a coolness subsisting between them for some time…

1 December 1780 – The people paraded, but the cold will not admit of much work. I spent the evening at – it is easy to guess where.

4 December 1780 – Mr. Cousin Simpson and Mr. Miles Prentice went to the Prerogative Office to take out a License, to bring me to the summet [sic] of my wishes, how impatiently I awaited their return, having my fears about me that His Excellency would interfere; an instance of the like happened but a short time since. They brought me notice that the instrument should be made out and sent to the Château the morning following to be signed, that I was to go to the office to take it up, etc. Still uneasy.

5 December 1780 – Went to Mr. Murray's office for the License, and being told that it was not returned from the Château, I was struck instantly with terror, confirmed as I thought in my former apprehensions. Told the Clerk with a faltering tongue, I should call again, went to the Cape, where I remained I don't know how for an hour; when I returned, and found to my great joy that my affair was completed, yet it was with great difficulty that I signed the Bond. Mr. Simpson spent the evening with me at Mr. Prentice's, and fixed on tomorrow evening for consummating my longing wishes.[137]

On 6 December 1780 James and Fanny were married in the home of Miles Prentice on Buade Street. Officiating at the ceremony was the Swiss-born rector of Quebec's Anglican church, DAVID-FRANÇOIS DE MONTMOLLIN. The Register Book entry reads:

No. 171. James Thompson, Overseer of the Works, widower of the Parish of Quebec, and Fanny Cooper, spinster of the same Parish, were married in this place by license this 6th day of December in the year 1780. By me David Francis de Montmollin, Rector. This marriage was solemnized between us. (signed) James Thompson and Fanny Cooper. In the presence of William Twiss, Commanding Engineer, Edward S. Salmon, Surgeon, and John Lynd.[138]

---

137. JTC.
138. Register book, Anglican Cathedral (Holy Trinity Church). Rev. de Montmollin used her nickname in the register book, rather than her given name (Frances). This document is further evidence that Thompson had been previously married.

Thompson, then forty-seven years of age, described the ceremony in his journal:

> 6 December 1780 – At six in the afternoon went to Mr. Prentice's where I met with my good friends Captain Twiss, and John Collins Esquire, being all that I asked to be present at the ceremony of my union with the never more to be called Miss Fanny Cooper. Parson Montmollin was particular to the time, and my happiness, as far as the law required, was accomplished.[139]

That Captain Lieutenant William Twiss,[140] was a witness to his marriage shows that Thompson's commanding officer was by now a good friend. Both were of simple yeoman origins and each recognized a kindred spirit and sense of professionalism in the other. At nineteen years of age, Twiss had been overseer of works at the mighty Gibraltar fortress, and in spite of the fact that Twiss's father had become rich and could afford to buy his boy's commission, their work was the common link between the two. Even so, affairs could take an unpleasant turn:

> 31 December 1780 – Busy all day, entering in a book alphabetically the endorsements on various vouchers, and papers, belonging to the Department throughout the Province. Received a note from Captain Twiss, blaming me very unjustly of neglect, but as he was ignorant of the cause of it at the time, the sting, with which it might otherwise bring, could not affect me.[141]

Now that he was married, it was time to stop inserting "amorous" entries into his official journal:

> 7 December 1780 – Visited the works in the afternoon, and after a short stay returned to my wife, brought her home to the Bishop's Palace after dark, accompanied by Mr. & Mrs. Prentice and Mr. Simpson. I have now done inserting here anything on my amorous subjects, and I trust in the good hand of Providence that this changing my condition will amply fulfill my expectations. It is now near four years since I was a single man, during which I was under the necessity of keeping house tho' I boarded with my cousin Simpson, having on account of my business, a numerous train of people daily after me, that no other family could put up with, and I must confess that I had no inclination to remain at home, farther than business obliged me, hardly ever thought of returning to it till my common time of rest, every evening throwing myself into company, to keep up my spirits … yet I must confess that Mrs. Simpson was not wanting in her endeavours to make everything as agreeable as possible, and often angry with me for passing my evening elsewhere.[142]

---

139. JTC.
140. The other witness was John Collins, Grand Master of the Ancient and Honourable Society of Free and Accepted Masons in Canada.
141. JTC.
142. *Ibid*. His comment that "it is now near four years since I was a single man," taken with

This journal entry is of interest on several accounts. One, he had been boarding with his cousin Alexander Simpson[143] for some time before his marriage, while at the same time maintaining his old residence on St. Louis Street as a "business office." Two, he appears to have been a lonely man (before he met Fanny) with no desire to remain for any time at his old residence, or at the Simpson's house, preferring to "throw himself into company to keep up his spirits." But the new "Mrs. Thompson" had changed all that.

The newly married couple set up their home in the Bishop's Palace, where Thompson had been given lodging the previous year. Interestingly, Thompson had decided not to take up residence in his home on St. Louis Street. Likely, he was renting it out to supplement his income.[144]

On 7 February 1781 Thompson woke up in the night with a severe pain in his chest. The following day, the pain was worse and he confined himself to his room. When the pain in his chest subsided, it was then replaced by a severe and persistent cough. On 13 February he was sick to his stomach. Concerned that his house confinement was "working against his health," he walked a little in the yard "in order to season myself to the open air, determined if I find myself tolerable to get to the Hill tomorrow [Cape Diamond], let the consequences be what it will." That night his cough returned, and he was unable to go to work the following day, but managed a short walk over to the Grand Battery. On the 15th he finally made it to the office, where he asked the clerks "if they did not find it warm, one of them said, he thought it warmer out of doors, returned to

---

his statement that he had buried General Richard Montgomery "just alongside of that of my first wife," has traditionally been interpreted that his wife was dead *before* the siege of Quebec, which was not the case. His letter to John Gawler (see footnote 105) proves that she was still alive on 21 May 1777 and highlights the tendency of Thompson's memory and oral storytelling techniques to confuse the historical record. The subject of his anecdote was not the burial of his wife, though in the retelling of the story her burial in close proximity to the American general took on an importance that was not related to the actual timing of her death. She is only mentioned in this anecdote because her final resting place gave him the crucial reference point he needed when tasked half a century later to disinter the general's body in 1818 and return it to the United States (see Chapter Nine). Thus he anachronistically included it in his oral narrative creating the impression that she was already "in the ground" at the time of Richard Montgomery's burial.

143. According to a census taken about 1773, Simpson was residing at Market Place in Lower Town. *Recensement de la population anglais demeurant à Québec vers 1773,* Archives du Séminaire de Québec, Polygraphie 37, No. 1.

144. JTC. Based on a journal entry dated 20 February 1784, Thompson had rented his St. Louis Street property "to the widow Watts at £19 a year, this is however falling £5 short of what it has brought this year, she is to take possession the 1st May next." Based on this entry, it is reasonable to assume that Thompson began to rent this property after he had moved in to the Bishop's Palace.

my room in a high fever with a strong palpitation at the heart. I laid down, and in about three hours after I recovered in great measure."[145]

The following day he found himself "in middling good spirits" and he ventured to the Cape "with an anxious wish to see the Works, being nine days absent from it." Likely a little surprised, he found all was well in spite of his lengthy absence. He soon returned home "and did not stir the rest of the day." By the 17th, his cough had just about left him but as the weather was poor he did not leave his house as he was "not thoroughly established in my health."[146]

One of Thompson's responsibilities as an overseer was to keep a sharp eye out for drunkenness, and likely as directed by garrison orders, he would fire anyone caught drinking on the job, and if a worker arrived at the site in this condition he immediately lost a day's pay. Thompson dreaded payday and with good reason. The workers, primarily soldiers from the garrison, were paid once a month, on a Saturday, and soldiers being soldiers, they quickly took advantage of the town's many inns and taverns:

> 21 February 1781 – Sergeant de Rettleberg [one of the German mercenaries] who was last summer the smartest & most useful among the sergeants, and intrusted with the checks of the foreign corps, has since through the means of drinking abused his trust, and lost to all sense of duty, was superseded in that office by Sergeant Mansback.[147]

On 27 March 1781 Thompson's cousin, Alexander Simpson, then sixty-three years of age, suddenly died and Thompson was forced to take time off from his heavy responsibilities on Cape Diamond to help Simpson's widow make funeral arrangements. "I was sent for in haste," he wrote, "from my cousin Simpson having been taken ill in the night which proved a heavy stroke of the apoplexy, and put an end to his existence at two in the afternoon, this stopped my going to the Hill the rest of the day.[148]

Simpson's remains were interred two days later:

> 29 March 1781 – … and the numerous train that conveyed it, from the first rank downwards, demonstrated how much he stood in the esteem public. The dis-

---

145. *Ibid.*
146. *Ibid.* It seems clear that Thompson had an infection (bacterial or viral) of some sort, as indicated by the fever, cough and stomach upset. He probably did not have access to a thermometer, so he may not have recorded accurately when his fever developed. Also, it is not clear where in the chest he had pains, but they seem to have been associated with lung rather than heart problems. From all of this we can reasonable conclude that he had some form of influenza.
147. *Ibid.* In 1830, between 400 and 500 liquor shops existed in Quebec, serving a population of scarcely 30,000 inhabitants, the military garrison included.
148. *Ibid.*

tress of his family is now great, and indeed their condition was alarming since the 1st of January last when Mrs. Simpson was taken ill...[149]

As indicated by the above journal entry, Simpson's wife, Sarah, had been seriously ill for the past three months and had

> underwent two desperate operations for an overgrown fistula in which her life was despaired of ... and my good friend & cousin was suddenly snatched away from her. Indeed the condition is really deplorable, the reflection on the loss of a dutiful husband is not the only difficulty she has to labour under, tho' in her present weakly condition is alone more than she is able to bear, but her large concern in trade will fall heavy on her without that assistance the head of her family naturally afforded.[150]

As a result, Thompson took on the responsibility to look out for the family and Simpson's daughter, Mary, would begin to look upon Thompson "in the light of a parent."[151]

That same year, Thompson was on the hunt across the province, for stone quarries for his many projects. He found a suitable quarry at Neuville, owned by Joseph Grenier, and he also found a source of good paving stones at L'Ange-Gardien. Other tasks that year included supervising construction of a dry-stone wall at the storehouse on Halstead's Wharf on Champlain Street, supervising work on Quebec's drainage system and supervising the repairs to the cellar of the Provost Prison in St. Roch suburb.

On 4 August 1781 Thompson and his old friend Michel Blais were summoned before Governor Haldimand to resolve some issues related to the "tract of unconceded [sic] land" which they had petitioned for some years back, and which "remains since filed in the Council Office of this Province waiting until lands may be granted." The issues involved land clearing and the use of the land to make hay. As Captain of Militia for the parish involved (St. Pierre), Blais had no objection to it being used to make hay, providing "it was the needy who reaped it," especially as the hay would be grown "near the poor people of these parishes." With regard to their long-standing application, Thompson and Blais were told that there were "numbers of Petitions filed in the Council Office, and that at peaceable times when lands would be granted, every one of them should have their due weight, and grants should be made out for the deserving at one and the same time."[152]

On 24 December 1781 Thompson shows up in official documents as the

---

149. *Ibid.*
150. *Ibid.*
151. *Ibid.*
152. *Ibid.*

town sergeant of the garrison.[153] Presumably this appointment was in addition to his duties as overseer of works in the Engineers Department. He remained as town sergeant at least until July 1783.

In July 1782 Thompson was ordered to investigate a claim against the government by Captain JAMES CUTHBERT, the seigneur of Berthier,[154] for damage to his lands caused by His Majesty's forces during the American Revolutionary War, especially "the Engineer's Department." The claim was not insignificant, amounting to £9,392 10s.[155] Armed with detailed written instructions from Twiss and accompanied by a notary, Thompson proceeded "post-haste" to Berthier and Sorel to conduct his investigation. It was a difficult assignment, one which required a delicate approach in dealing with local militia and law enforcement officers, and fraught with political overtones, but Thompson eventually proved that the claim was unjustified, in fact that total losses suffered by Cuthbert amounted to only £69 17s 7d.[156] On 17 July 1782, Thompson forwarded a copy of his final report to Governor Haldimand.

At 8 o'clock in the morning on 14 September 1782, Thompson was working on Cape Diamond when a messenger delivered an urgent message from Fanny, telling him to get home as quickly as possible. The happy couple's first child, William, was born as the clock struck twelve. It was a difficult birth, but Fanny and the baby got through the ordeal apparently in good condition. However, nine days later, Fanny took a turn for the worst:

> 23 September 1782 – In going home to dinner I found my wife in a worse condition than I left her in, having a high fever, which caused a most violent headache, and her breasts very hard, this last I considered a forerunner of sore breasts from which I pray God to avert, having had in my first wife a fatal experience! I ran immediately for the Doctor who applied honey and flannel to her breasts, and gave her something to drink.[157]

---

153. "Returns of the Staff of the Garrison," Quebec, 24 December 1781; 24 December 1782; 24 June 1783. LAC, RG 8 "C" Series, British Military & Naval Records, Microfilm C-10861. At this time Quebec was still a garrison town under military control. Over this same period, the garrison's provost marshal (in effect, the garrison's chief of police) was Miles Prentice, the former provost marshal in Wolfe's army (who had married the aunt of Thompson's wife).
154. Cuthbert had claimed that the army had cut timber on his lands without his authorization and had built a bridge across the River Berthier where he had an exclusive right to ferry.
155. Captain William Twiss to General Frederick Haldimand, Quebec, 16 July 1782, LAC, *Sessional Papers* (No. 6B) 53 Victoria, A.1890, 116. In July 1828, Thompson remembered the amount as £10,000 "less two shillings and six pence." (See Appendix A, "Memorandum of the most arduous services…").
156. This should be read: 69 pounds, 17 shillings, 7 pence.
157. JTC.

Based on this journal entry, both of Thompson's wives had infectious mastitis, a not uncommon affliction of nursing mothers.[158] Although 18th-century medicine was abysmally bad – bleeding, purging, etc. – and often worse than useless, most women did survive this affliction, at least in the milder cases. Thompson's first wife was one of the unlucky ones.

On 29 September William was baptised by the Reverend George Henry in the Thompson residence, "in the presence of Mrs. Sarah Simpson, the Granny, Messrs. Miles Prentice, John Lynd, Samuel Henry, & Hugh McKay." Fanny was still feeling "poorly."[159]

Late in 1782 Thompson learned that two convicted felons would be executed in Quebec. Based on the following entry in his journal, it is unlikely that he chose to be an eyewitness to the event:

> 18 November 1782 – This day two fellows were executed for the murder and robbery of Captain Stead, commander of one of the Treasury brigs, on the evening on the 31 December 1779, between the Upper and the Lower Town. The criminals went through Port St. Louis, about 11 o'clock, at a slow and doleful pace, to the place where justice had allotted them to suffer the most ignominious death. It is astonishing to see what a crowd of people followed the tragic scene. Even our people on the works (Cape Diamond) prayed Captain Twiss for leave to follow the hard-hearted crowd.[160]

Early in the following year, Thompson's precious little "Billy" became quite ill, perhaps a result of the difficulty which Fanny experienced while nursing her son. He wrote dejectedly: "My child is still very ill, and has every appearance of death about him. To his fate I must submit, but I dread the effect it is likely to have on his disconsolate mother."[161] On the following day, he added, "My child is drawing near the end of its existence." The Thompson's "little Billy" passed away a few days later on 2 March 1783 "and at five in the evening his remains were interred alongside my cousin Simpson."[162]

---

158. Infectious mastitis is caused by a bacterial infection, which if untreated can develop into an abscess or sepsis. The modern treatment is a course of antibiotics. The main cure at that time would be the woman's own immune system fighting off the underlying cause, the infection.
159. JTC. A military chaplain at the time of the Conquest, the Rev. George Henry became Quebec's first civilian Presbyterian minister in Quebec in 1765 when regular services began in a room in the Jesuits' College. He died in Quebec on 6 July 1795, aged eighty-six years.
160. *Ibid.* Also, Lemoine, *Picturesque Quebec*, 259.
161. *Ibid.*
162. *Ibid.* Thompson's cousin, Alexander "Sanders" Simpson, had died of a stroke on 27 March 1781.

James and Fanny would have eight other children, two of whom, like Billy, died in infancy. The six children who survived infancy were:[163]

> JAMES, born 27 March 1784;
> ANNE "NANCY," born 9 January 1786;
> WILLIAM ALEXANDER, born 7 January 1787;
> JOHN GAWLER, born 7 January 1787;
> GEORGE, born 5 July 1789; and
> FRANCES "FANNY," born 11 June 1798.

On 24 October 1783 Thompson said his goodbyes to his best friend, Captain Twiss, "a most disagreeable task ... yet it is pleasing to reflect that parting was attended with a mutual regret."[164] Thompson now had to begin a "fresh score" with Lieutenant HENRY RUDYERD,[165] his new commanding engineer, noting in his journal, "I hope and indeed it is my wish as my interest to please him as I have done the rest of the black cuffs."[166] With the temporary citadel essentially complete, Twiss had been given permission to return to his young wife in England – he had married only nine months previous to his arrival in North America in the spring of 1776 – and to begin work on the fortifications of Portsmouth. He was eventually replaced as chief engineer in Quebec by GOTHER MANN.[167]

The following summer, Haldimand was recalled back to England,[168] a particularly hard pill for Thompson to swallow, as Haldimand was not only a fellow veteran of the Seven Years' War but a firm supporter of Thompson and his family. This is evidenced by the glowing recommendation which Haldimand left to

---

163. James Jr. and William Alexander went into the commissariat service; John Gawler became a lawyer and was later appointed a judge in Gaspé; George initially entered the commissariat service, but later attended the Royal Military Academy at Woolwich and on graduation, obtained an officers' commission in the Royal Artillery; Frances married a physician and surgeon, and Anne married a prosperous merchant. It is interesting to note that James Jr. left a memorandum detailing his life and that of his three brothers but left no mention of his two sisters, noting "nothing remarkable being attached to the history of the female branch." Besides William, two other children died as infants: Samuel (1792); and Rose (1793–97).
164. JTC.
165. Rudyerd left Quebec on 15 August 1785.
166. JTC. At this time, officers of the Corps of Engineers wore blue coats with black velvet facings (lapels, cuffs and standing collar), thus the colloquial term "black cuffs." About 1811, to avoid confusion with French officers, they adopted scarlet coats with blue facings.
167. Gother Mann arrived in Quebec in May 1785 and was commanding engineer in Canada until 1791, and then again from 1794 to 1804, when he was replaced by Lieutenant Colonel Ralph Henry Bruyères.
168. While Haldimand was recalled back to England in the summer of 1784, it was two years before a successor was appointed (the lieutenant governor, Henry Hope, assumed his responsibilities). His successor was Guy Carleton, now known as Baron Dorchester.

his successors in an attempt to have Thompson retained in his post, despite the cuts that came with the return of peace:[169]

> This is to certify that the Bearer hereof, Mr. James Thompson, having been employed as Overseer of Works in the Engineer Department at this place since the year 1772, has been recommended to me by the Officers under whom he served for his attention and fidelity. And having discharged his duty to my satisfaction during my Command, and being an old and faithful servant of the Crown, I have thought fit to continue him in his present employment, and do hereby recommend him to the favour and protection of all officers who may hereafter succeed to this Command.[170]

Thompson had an equally high opinion of General Haldimand, as indicated by the following journal entry:

> 10 November 1784 – His Excellency has left behind him some friends and many enemies, how far he misled their ill will, I cannot pretend to say, but I am clear in it, he has done more for the Public good than all his predecessors put together. He was free of access, indefatigable in business, never trusting to his servants in office in settling even the most trifling business of government, but saw it down himself and that with the greatest dispatch. He was a perfect judge in all branches of mechanical business, these are characters which every one allows him, and from such qualifications I revere him, and sincerely wish he may get the better of all those that falsely accuse him.[171]

In November 1783 Thompson completed unauthorized alterations to his apartment in the Bishop's Palace, shortening the long passage between his dining room and kitchen, "which rendered the victuals before they reach any table hardly fit to eat in the winter." As a possible defence, he had consulted with the Advocate General (who had lodgings and offices in the same building) "who approved on the propriety of having it [done] on seeing the convenience it would afford."[172]

On 22 November 1783 James and Fanny were witnesses to the marriage of their good friend LAUCHLAN SMITH,[173] the seigneur of St. Ann parish, and Bar-

---

169. The Treaty of Paris, signed on 3 September 1783 (ratified by the U.S. Congress on 14 January 1784), formally ended the American Revolutionary War, although the last British troops only left New York City on 25 November 1783. These staff cuts must have abolished the position of Edward Burford, the other overseer of works.
170. JTC. See also "James Thompson Fonds," LAC, MG23-K2, Microfilm M-2312 (original documents held at BAnQ). This microfilm includes Thompson's letter-book of anecdotes, parts of his work-related journals, as well as miscellaneous documents and correspondence.
171. JTC.
172. *Ibid.*
173. Lauchlan Smith, a former sergeant in Fraser's Highlanders, had become a prosperous merchant in Quebec, and later the seigneur of St. Ann parish.

bra Boyton, one of Fanny's cousins. The ceremony took place at the home of Miles Prentice.[174] Early in 1784 Thompson lost another good friend when Captain CHARLES GRANT died suddenly (the gentleman who had given Thompson his first snuff mull – see Anecdote 32):

> 7 January 1784 – I was this morning suddenly surprised with the melancholy news of the death of my good friend Mr. Charles Grant of this City merchant, who breathed his last at this day at noon, and left behind him a wife and five young ones. From his public spirit his decease is become a public loss – the Labourious [sic] class of men will sensibly feel it, many of whom he employed constantly and paid daily, or as their wants required.[175]

On the 16th Thompson attended Grant's funeral and mentions the Masonic procession, of which he obviously was a part, which attended the interment:

> He was for some years Treasurer for the Provincial Grand Lodge, and the General Fund of Charity, a steady member of Merchants Lodge No. 1. The whole Fraternity at this place paid his remains their tribute of their regard, by following it in Procession with their regalia to the place of interment, which made a very respectable appearance, which with the numerous citizens from the highest to the lower class, demonstrated how much he was beloved.[176]

Thompson, now in his early fifties, was starting to show the effects of the many years spent outdoors, exposed to all kinds of weather. In early 1784 he experienced his first bout with rheumatism:

> 9 February 1784 – In putting on my surtout coat in the morning,[177] I was struck a severe pain in my left shoulder, and supposed I had hurt my shoulder in hauling on the sleeve. I was in great torment with it till towards evening, but when I went to bed, it returned upon me, so that I could stir from one position all night, and concluded it was a touch of the Rheumatism, which I thank God I have not felt before.[178]

But of greater concern was the return of his persistent cough:

> 19 February 1784 – I struggled hard and in a severe cough all this day, which increases fast upon me, and disturbed me much in the night, fall asleep towards

---

174. *Ibid*.
175. *Ibid*. In Anecdote 32, Thompson discusses the snuff mull which Charles Grant had given him.
176. *Ibid*.
177. *Ibid*. A surtout coat was an overcoat resembling a frock coat (from French, *sur* over + *tout* all).
178. *Ibid*. It is also possible that Thompson suffered from "referred pain" and not rheumatism. Myocardial ischaemia (the loss of blood flow to a part of the heart muscle tissue) is possibly the best known example of referred plain; the sensation can occur in the upper chest as a restricted feeling, or as an ache in the left shoulder, arm or hand.

morning and from the fatigue of it, did not awake till it was too late for the morning Parade, which I have not missed for many months before.

21 February 1784 – My cough has once more prevented my getting in time to the Cape [for morning call], indeed to my remembrances I never felt the like of it. It tears me to pieces, my very internals are sore with straining, and can get no rest in the night from its effects. I am convinced it is what is called the hooping cough,[179] is common in this place among the youth, but I am told there are several worse than myself that has got it.

23 February 1784 – My cough has now got so far master of me that I must yield to it and (malgre moi) stay at home. I can have no rest for it in the nights. In the day it is somewhat moderate, but so soon as I lay my head on the pillow, it begins furiously and tears me to pieces all the night long, by which I disturb my wife's rest, which adds to my troubles.[180]

On 27 March 1784 Fanny gave birth to another son, James Jr., and after Divine service on Sunday, 4 April, Reverend George Henry baptised the boy in their lodging at the Bishop's Palace "in the presence of Lauchlan Smith, Esquire, Seigneur of St. Ann, Miles Prentice, and his son Lieutenant Samuel Prentice of the 84th Regiment."[181]

It wasn't until 22 April that Thompson finally "turned off" his great coat and fur cap for the first time this season, "nor would I keep them on so long only for my cough, which has not yet parted with me, tho' it attacks me but at long intervals."[182]

Ever since his good friend Captain Twiss had left Canada, Thompson had been seeking to have his job transferred to the Ordnance Department, and he sent two letters to Twiss to see if he could pull any strings. On 13 June 1784 he received the following response:

> My private affairs will not permit me to return to Canada, nor is any commanding engineer yet appointed to that station. Indeed the repeated changes in the Great Political have greatly retarded any general arrangement in all Departments, amongst others nothing fixed on for Quebec, but I have taken case to lay before his Grace the Duke of Richmond, the particulars of your services at Quebec, and by doing this in writing, and in an official manner, I have no

---

179. Whooping cough, or *pertussis*, is an infection of the respiratory system. It is characterized by severe coughing spells that end in a "whooping" sound when the person breathes in. Before the development of a vaccine in the 1920s, *pertussis* killed about 10,000 people in North America annually.
180. JTC.
181. *Ibid*. Interestingly, the official baptismal entry in St. Andrew's Church register, 10 April 1784, shows that the baptism was witnessed by Lauchlan Smith *and John Lynd* (a merchant in Quebec).
182. *Ibid*.

doubt from his Grace's attention to business, but you will be treated in the way your merit deserves, and should it ever be in my power to promote your interest, you may depend on my endeavour to do it effectively.[183]

Governor Haldimand had divided his time between the Château Saint-Louis[184] and a new building he had commissioned next to Place d'Armes by the old ramparts, just below today's Château Frontenac. The cornerstone of the new three-storey building, known as Château Haldimand (or Haldimand Castle), was laid on 5 May 1784 and it was completed in 1787. It was used as a vice-regal residence, council room for the Legislature and for other government purposes.[185]

In 1784, during the course of this work, Thompson's workers discovered a large stone with an engraved Maltese cross bearing the date 1647, part of the original Château Saint-Louis:

> 17 September 1784 – The miners at the Chateau in levelling the yard, dug up a large stone from which I have described the attached figure. I could wish it was discovered soon enough to lay conspicuously in the wall of the New Building (Haldimand Castle), in order to convey to posterity the antiquity of the Château St. Louis. However, I got the masons to lay the stone in the cheek of the gate of the new building.[186]

The garrison's parade ground, or Esplanade, was laid out between 1779 and 1783 when work was progressing on the temporary citadel. In addition to its function as a military parade ground, it provided an effective defensive function by creating a greater distance between the walled-in part of the city and the ramparts. In a 25 October 1784 journal entry, Thompson was not impressed by its high construction costs: "cost government much labour & expense in blowing down rocks, filling up quarry pits & levelling the place for public utility."[187]

On 30 December 1784 Thompson associated himself with the son of Michel Blais (also called Michel) and they made another joint application for land in

---

183. *Ibid.* William Twiss to James Thompson, London, 30 March 1874.
184. The first château was built by Governor Montmagny in 1648 and by the late 1680s it had fallen into an advanced state of disrepair. A replacement was started by Governor Frontenac in 1694, building on the foundation of the former château, with a new pavilion and two wings added between 1719 and 1723. Located on the top of a cliff, it was a choice target for British gunners in 1759. By 1766 it had fallen into ruins. The southern sections were repaired, followed by the northern section in 1798.
185. Château Haldimand was demolished in 1892 to make way for the Château Frontenac.
186. JTC. The stone was engraved with a Maltese cross, enclosed within a shield, and bore the date "1647."
187. *Ibid.* When level, the land was simply planted with grass and dotted with a few trees. Intersecting pathways completed the Esplanade's landscaping. While intended as a military parade ground, it was often used by civilians for picnics, lacrosse matches, foot races and other sports.

Château Haldimand, 1830. Detail of Image 6, page 106 (see "A Colour Album"). On 5 May 1784 Governor Frederick Haldimand lay the cornerstone of a new official residence, Château Haldimand, with James Thompson in charge of the miners and masons during its construction. When completed in 1787, it was inaugurated by Haldimand's successor, Lord Dorchester. It remained the residence for British governors until 1811, when it housed military and civil offices. The building served Laval Normal School in the later 19th century until its demolition in 1892 to make way for the Château Frontenac Hotel. Watercolour by James Pattison Cockburn. (Royal Ontario Museum 942.48.87)

Armagh County, but this time with the assistance of the former governor, Haldimand, by then in England:

> Your Petitioner therefore humbly prays, that in justice to the family of the deceased Michel Blais, your Honours may be pleased to consider Michel Blais in this and the former petition as in the place and stead of his deceased father, and grant to your petitioner and him, the said tract of land, as described and set forth in the said petition of the 9th February 1779....[188]

---

188. *Ibid*. Petition dated 30 December 1784. Michel Blais, Thompson's friend and former landlord, had died on 5 September 1783. As a result, Thompson's earlier joint application for a land grant, which had still not been approved, suddenly became invalid.

In spite of Haldimand's glowing testament to his services, Thompson still felt insecure as his job continued to remain on a temporary footing. On 2 August 1785 he received a letter from William Twiss telling him that a new position of Ordnance Department barrack-master had been set up in Quebec and was still unfilled. Thompson applied for the position to the Duke of Richmond,[189] then Master General of the Ordnance, and attached a "memorial" which described his past fourteen years of service. The following journal entry shows that he didn't have much hope for the appointment, but he hoped at least that his current position might be confirmed by Warrant:

> 25 October 1785 – ... but lest a disappointment should be the case, which is most likely, and that I might not give up my pretension to the place I have held for fourteen years past, my prayer is for the former, or, a confirmation in the latter, which for want of a Warrant from the Master General made by enjoyment of it but on a temporary footing. In this memorial I have set forth my services under every Engineer since the conquest in 1759, and referred his Grace to Generals Haldimand, Sir Guy Carleton and Murray, Colonel William Spry, and Captain Twiss under whom I served for my character, and took the liberty to the two first Generals on the subject of my memorial, in order to prepare them, in case his Grace should question them about me. If he does, I have every reason to think they will do me justice.[190]

On 15 August 1785 Captain Rudyerd, Thompson's Commanding Engineer, departed Quebec. "I never yet parted with a Commanding Officer without regret," Thompson observed in his journal, adding that Rudyerd had been "very civil to me during his Command here."[191]

The period from the end of September until the middle of October 1785 saw a strange weather occurrence in Quebec, its chief characteristics being darkness, fog, haze and frequent rain. The climax to this unusual phenomenon occurred on 16 October, popularly known as the "Dark Day of Canada," for the darkness extended across a large portion of the country.[192] The following account was entered in Thompson's journal:

> Sunday, 16 October 1785 – Weather hazy and dark in the morning, which increased so that candles were necessary to be lighted in Church at noon, without which the Service could not be performed. About one, rain came on accompanied with thunder & lightning, the darkness increasing the phenomenon

---

189. Charles Lennox, Duke of Richmond. See Charles Lennox for Biographical Note.
190. JTC.
191. *Ibid.*
192. J.-M. Lemoine, *Quebec Past and Present: A History of Quebec, 1608–1876* (Quebec, 1876), Appendix: H.H. Miles, "Dark Days of Canada, 1785." See also, Jonathan Sewell, "A Few Notes upon the Dark Days of Canada," LHSQ, *Transactions*, Original Series, vol 2 (1831).

became wonderful and, a striking awe, at two o'clock so dark as could be seen in the silent hour of midnight, and not a soul to be found in the streets, the cows belonging to the Town seemingly frightened quit their pasture and hasted away home – a glimpse of light now and then between 2 and 4, so that one could see if any walked in the streets. At 4, total darkness again, and a very extraordinary clap of thunder, which shaked our people in the old Citadel most sensibly (as they say) such a stench of sulphur as was like to stifle them. The water in their tubs under the eave-spouts got as black as ink, and they allude this to the Cannon of the Garrison (laying on sheds near the house) having attracted the lightning, however in this, they were partly mistaken, for the water appeared black everywhere particularly that exposed to the air; in short everything appeared dismal, and all that have seen it, may with propriety say that they passed one night in their life of thirty-six hours, and it is the first, that I eat my dinner at two o'clock in the day with candle light.[193]

On 9 January 1786 Thompson recorded a happier event in his journal, "My wife brought to bed of a daughter at 11 o'clock P.M." This was followed on 15 January with, "My daughter, baptized Nancy, by the Reverend Mr. Henry."[194]

During the winter of 1785–86, Thompson's persistent cough returned with a vengeance:

27 February 1786 – Much troubled with the cough all day. I was the same in the night, what sleep I had at short intervals did me no great good, being accompanied by unpleasant dreams.

28 February 1786 – No alteration in my condition for the better, and I dread the nights, always watching and wishing for daylight. Confinement frets me exceedingly, Cape Diamond is my hobbytown, never satisfied when anything prevents my being there.

1 March 1786 – Last night afforded more rest than I have had for some nights past, yet I had a great share of coughing but did not tear one as usual, and I think it lighter in the course of the day … by it my spirits is quite low … and would have been more so had I not been relieved in some degree by the visits of my friends. Now I am a little diverted by seeing numbers of skating on the ice as well as passing to and from Point Levy.[195]

---

193. JTC. So-called "dark days" have been recorded for centuries. Usually there is a gradual increasing gloom until it becomes so dark that artificial light is necessary. This darkness may last a few hours or several days and decrease as gradually as it came. New England and the southern portions of eastern Canada are the regions in North America which have experienced the greatest frequency of dark days in the past two centuries. Most dark days in Canada have been caused by forest and prairie fires. In other countries peat fires and volcanic eruptions have been the primary cause.
194. *Ibid.*
195. *Ibid.*

Meanwhile, Captain Gother Mann, the new Commanding Engineer in Canada, was busy formulating a new defensive plan, one that gave priority to finishing Quebec's ramparts along the cliff, along with the addition of new auxiliary defensive works. One such project was Hope Gate, on the northern face of the ramparts, the first purely British gate built in Quebec.[196] When construction started in 1786, Thompson was put in charge of the masons and stone layers:

> 12 April 1786 – Some days since the Commanding Engineer received orders from General Hope to build a gate of ten feet wide where the Sally Port is called by the Canadians Port du Conotrie, the inhabitants of that quarter of the Town, within and without side the Fortification having Petitioned him for that indulgence for the conveniency of carriages going and coming that way, and they to get a cart road made from that gate to the water side at their own joint expense – and by way of a beginning to this business, the masons, two labourers, and four horses, were this day employed in taking stones from St. Roch to the Sally Port.[197]

Over the winter of 1785–86, Quebec's citizens were stricken with a particularly lethal strain of influenza, which seemed to affect "the fair sex at a certain age." According to Thompson, it "seizes the glands of the neck and swells to such a degree that they are strangled by it."[198] Thompson would know of these effects from a personal standpoint, as *la grippe* managed to kill one of his distant relatives:

> 12 June 1786 – I had a young girl of about 14 years, a distant relation taken ill with this cruel disorder on the evening of the 28 January last, sent for the Doctor who advised her being removed to his house without delay, that the necessary attention for her disorder may be given, which she could not have at home, my wife being in child bed. This was done, and I hired two women to attend her at a dollar each per night, and notwithstanding every care and attention she died the fourth night. On her death bed she declared herself a Roman Catholic, and was interred according to the ceremony of that Church. This disorder is attended with the Scarlet Fever, and while it continued in its vigour, funeral processions were seen in the streets every hour of the day.[199]

---

196. The 1745 *enceinte* built by the French had only three gates: St. Louis and St. John on the western side (facing the Plains of Abraham) and Palace on the northern side. At the end of the 18th century the British built two additional gates: Hope, in 1786; and Prescott, in 1797. Hope was also located on the northern side, while Prescott closed the road between Lower and Upper Towns (Côte de la Montagne).
197. JTC.
198. *Ibid.*
199. *Ibid.* The identity of this "distant relative" is unknown but it was likely one of his wife's relations.

Hope Gate. Named for Lieutenant Governor Henry Hope, the gate was erected in 1786 at the request of the French Canadians, who wanted easier access between the rapidly growing St. Roch suburb and Upper Town's market place. It was the first purely British gate built in Quebec, and James Thompson oversaw the masons and stone layers during construction. As can be seen in these two views, architectural features on the interior façade (bottom image) differ from those on the exterior (top image). For example, the pediment's bull's-eye window on the exterior side is replaced by a rectangular block of stone (with a Latin inscription) on the interior. Also, on the interior side, the cut-stone trim frames only the flattened arch. Top, photograph c.1871 (Editor's Collection); bottom, watercolour by James Pattison Cockburn, 1830. (LAC R-9266-138)

As evidenced by the following journal entry, Thompson was unhappy with his masons, still working to complete Hope Gate:

> 9 September 1786 – This afternoon the masons finished laying the Facia to the gate. I think it was high time, tho' in fact it could be no sooner reasonably expected, not only from the [number of] hands we have got, but from our not having cut stone ready before hand to bring us forward. We have seven hands at it, four of them are military men who can hardly be called half-bred masons, and one of our three civilians is only a stone layer. Thus, when we have a course of stones cut we lay it, and set to cutting another, which makes the work exceedingly tedious. I am persuaded it will take us till some time in November, before we can close the pediment. The French inhabitants, in compliment to the commander in chief, have requested to have something inscribed on a stone in this pediment to perpetuate his memory for his readiness in condescending to give the people a Gate in this quarter.[200]

That same month, Thompson's two children were inoculated for smallpox – perhaps the recent influenza epidemic had focused his thoughts on the health of his family. On 27 September 1786 he wrote : "This morning my two young ones, James and Nancy were inoculated for the small Pox by Doctor Latham, the famous inoculator."[201]

The appointment as Governor of the Province of Quebec remained vacant until 23 October 1786 when Guy Carleton, now Lord Dorchester, replaced Haldimand (who had vacated the appointment two years previously).[202] The garrison turned out under arms to welcome Carleton back, lining the streets of Quebec between the Château and the landing place in Lower Town. Amidst sa-

---

200. *Ibid.* See also, Lemoine, *Quebec Past and Present*, 352.
201. *Ibid.* Before Edward Jenner pioneered the use of the safer cowpox vaccine, the technique of variolation, or "smallpox inoculation," was in use. This involved rubbing liquid from a smallpox pustule into a small scratch on the arm, which produced a mild reaction and a lifelong immunity. Dr. James Latham was a former British army surgeon, and the first person to have practised inoculation for smallpox in Canada. He came to Canada with his regiment in July 1768 and undertook inoculation in Quebec and Montreal in the years 1768–70 and again in 1786. In 1786 his advertisement as an inoculator appeared in the *Quebec Gazette* from 28 September to 30 November, so this fits well with Thompson's claim that his two children were inoculated on 29 September. Latham's treatment was expensive, in the order of £3, so it was limited to prominent families, although his fee could be adjusted to the financial circumstances of the patient. Thompson is silent on how much he paid Latham for the two procedures.
202. In the 1780s, the British government accepted the idea that the provinces of Quebec, Nova Scotia and New Brunswick should share a single governor-in-chief (afterwards termed the governor general). The first individual to occupy this office was Guy Carleton, Lord Dorchester, appointed in 1785. However, the governor general only directly governed the province of Lower Canada; Upper Canada, New Brunswick and Nova Scotia were instead headed by their own lieutenant governors.

lutes from both the attending frigate and the Grand Battery, Carleton walked to the Château, where he was immediately sworn into office. As a mark of respect, that night every house was illuminated. Thompson had intended to pay his respects to Carleton but thought it best to wait until the various ceremonies attended by the "great folks" had ended. However, Carleton surprised Thompson by sending for him:

> 30 October 1786 – It has been my intention since the arrival of His Excellency Guy Lord Dorchester to pay him my respects, but not before the hurry of that sort of ceremony was chiefly over by the Great Folks, however his Lordship took the start of me this morning by sending for me, when he was pleased to see that I looked younger than when he saw me last. I returned the compliment, in saying that however young I looked, I was persuaded that I did not appear so young as his Lordship. He then informed me that he was distressed for want of room in the Château to accommodate his servants, etc., and that he sent for me in order to have a thorough survey of the building, to make as much conveniency in it as it could admit – then went with him through every apartment even into the kitchen cellars, and out houses. He visited also the new building [Château Haldimand], which, he seemed to admire tho' (says he) its outside appearance was not so flattering.… On this occasion I was informed by Major Mathews, that as many repairs and jobs would be wanted in and about the Château it was settled by his Lordship and the Commanding Engineer, that the application should be to me by one of the aides de camp, and if the business required, was but triffling, to order it immediately, and if of some consequence first to inform the Commander of it, and I to receive his directions concerning it. That I was not to do anything at the request of any of the servants even if they made use of his Lordships authority.[203]

Early in 1787 Thompson received bad news about his firewood allotment, which led to the news that he would have to vacate his apartments in the Bishop's Palace:

> 13 January 1787 – This day I called at the Barrack Masters office where I was informed that half of my firewood was cut off in the new regulation. From thence, went to General Hope, told him it was impossible for me to pass a winter in the Bishop's Palace with an allowance of half a cord of wood, that I had double that since 1767 and he was pleased to say that it was contrary he would be obliged to me for removing, as government had use for the apartments I occupied, told the General that I had no objections to quit as early in the spring as he pleased, but that readjusting the fire wood I thought extremely hard. To this he said he would endeavour to continue the old allowance till April next.[204]

---

203. JTC.
204. *Ibid.*

Thompson received more bad news on 25 March 1787 when he learned that his "extra pay" (two shillings and six pence) had been terminated by Governor Carleton, who took the position that extra pay in time of peace was unprecedented. With Thompson's growing family (by now, they had two children and Fanny was pregnant again), this substantial deduction in his pay created particular hardships. Thompson had started to receive lodging money in January 1788, so it would appear that he had vacated his Bishop's Palace apartment by the end of 1787, as intimated by General HENRY HOPE,[205] possibly moving into his house on St. Louis Street.

In June 1787 Miles Prentice, an old friend and fellow Freemason, passed away. For some years, his widow continued to operate Free Mason's Hall, eventually selling it to Quebec's Freemasons. At this point it appears she moved in with the Thompson family (she was the aunt of Fanny, Thompson's wife).

On 21 August 1787 Carleton put on a grand pyrotechnic display for Prince William Henry, Duke of Clarence, the young "sailor prince," who had arrived in Quebec on the warship *Pegasus* a few days previously.[206] Once again, Thompson was involved with the event, albeit in his construction role:

> Monday, 21 August 1787 – I have received his Lordship's (Lord Dorchester) orders to erect a platform on the roof of a vaulted house, originally a powder magazine, joining to the upper end of the new building, [Haldimand Castle] for His Royal Highness (Prince William Henry) and his company to sit upon while the fireworks are displaying on an eminence fronting it below the old Citadel.[207]

On 7 January 1788 Thompson was startled when his servant girl arrived at the office to tell him that his wife was ill. He ran home and was immediately convinced that help was required without delay. "I made the greatest speed to Lower Town for Doctor Lajuste,[208] then to St. John Street in Upper Town for the nurse," explained Thompson, and after repeatedly running out to speed the nurse on her way, he arrived home to learn that his wife had just delivered a child "between one & two o'clock." He then ran to tell his good friend, Sarah Simpson, "whose indisposition could not admit of her coming," and when he returned home again, he was told "there was another child born since I went out." After some time in suspense, he was told that Fanny had delivered two boys. On 13 January the new twins were baptised William Alexander and John

---

205. Colonel Henry Hope. A career military officer, Hope had been sworn in as lieutenant governor of Quebec on 2 November 1785 and acted as governor in Haldimand's absence.
206. Prince William was the third son of George III and the future King William IV.
207. JTC.
208. Dr. Louis-François Lajus. See Part Three for Biographical Note.

Gawler "in the presence of Mr. John Lynd, Mr. John Fraser, Mr. John Ross & Mr. James Gricy."[209]

On 5 July 1789 Fanny gave birth to another son, George, their fifth child who would survive.[210] By 1791 they were residing at 34 St. Louis Street, likely the same house he had purchased with General Murray's approval back in 1760.[211]

On 22 September 1791 Thompson purchased a 50 × 90-foot parcel of land (Cadaster Number 2715) on the corner of St. Ursula Street and Ursulines Lane (rue Sainte-Ursule and ruette des Ursulines). The land was purchased from Charles Cornélier *dit* Grandchamp, who had acquired the land two years earlier from the Ursuline nuns. Thompson's new stone house would be built in the traditional "English" architectural style introduced in Lower Canada by British architects. The house would be built to a rectangular plan with its main entrance fronting on Ursulines Lane, in stark contrast to neighbouring houses, which would have their principal entrances on St. Ursula Street.[212] With a slightly raised ground floor over a full basement, the impressive structure would rise two and half storeys, all topped with a gable roof. Nine attic windows would provide light to its upper rooms. It is likely that Thompson prepared his own building plans, but we can be sure that he carefully supervised its construction. His impressive new house would take nearly eight years to build, no doubt because of his limited financial resources.[213]

On 26 December 1791 the Parliament of Great Britain divided the Province of Quebec into two parts corresponding to their location on the St. Lawrence River: the western half became Upper Canada (now southern Ontario) while the eastern half became Lower Canada (now southern Quebec). Known as the Constitutional Act of 1791, this measure was enacted to accommodate the many English-speaking settlers, known as United Empire Loyalists, who had arrived from the United States following the American Revolutionary War. Upper Canada received English law and institutions, while Lower Canada retained French law and institutions, including seigneurial land tenure, and the privileges accorded to the Roman Catholic Church. Representative governments were estab-

---

209. *Ibid.*
210. The family now consisted of James, Fanny and five children: James Jr.; Nancy; the twins William Alexander and John Gawler; and George.
211. 1791 Directory of Quebec. Honorius Provost, *Les Premiers Anglo-Canadiens à Québec: Essai de recensement 1759–1775*, Institut québécois de recherche sur la culture (Quebec, 1984).
212. The entrance fronting on Ursulines Lane would be condemned in the second half of the 19th century.
213. It is possible that Thompson sold his house and lot on St. Louis Street to help finance the new construction.

lished in both colonies with the creation of a legislative assembly (Quebec had not previously had representative government).

On 5 February 1792 Fanny gave birth to another son, Samuel. Little is known of this child except that he died at a very young age. On 22 July 1793 she then gave birth to another daughter, Rose. Again, little is known of this child except that she died on 18 April 1797.

Sometime before the end of July 1792 the Thompson family had moved to 11 Angel Street (rue des Anges). In that year the curé of Quebec's Upper Town conducted a parish census which included the name of the head of each household as well as the number of parishioners and communions (those who received communion). The entry in the 1792 Parish Census for rue des Anges in Haute-ville (Upper Town) reads: "No. 11 – Sergeant Thompson, 1 parishioner; 1 communion."[214] This census data shows that Thompson still retained the services of a live-in Roman Catholic housekeeper (the single parishioner who also took communion). Meanwhile construction of his new house on St. Ursula Street slowly progressed.

On 17 June 1794 Thompson, now in his early sixties, was given an assistant, Richard Goldsworthy. With the title of Assistant Overseer of Works, Goldsworthy was paid two shillings and six pence per day, along with an annual lodging allowance of £12. In 1795 the Royal Engineers[215] Department in Quebec consisted of:[216]

> ENGINEER'S DEPARTMENT IN UPPER AND LOWER CANADA, QUEBEC, 1795
> Gother Mann, Lieut. Colonel, Commanding Engineer
> Benjamin Fisher, Captain
> Alexander Bryce, 1st Lieutenant
> Thomas Lacey, 2nd Lieutenant
> William Hall, Draughts-man
> James Thompson, Overseer of Works

On 15 May 1798 the curé of the Upper Town conducted another parish census, and like the census of 1792, it included the name of the head of each household as well as the number of parishioners and communions at each residence. But the 1798 census also included the number of Protestants in each household. The 1798 Parish Census entry for ruette des Ursulines, Haute-Ville reads: "No. 5

---

214. This particular parish census, taken on 30 July 1792, did not include any additional information on Protestants – understandable, as they were not part of the priest's responsibilities.
215. In April 1787, the Corps of Engineers was granted the "Royal" prefix, becoming the Corps of Royal Engineers.
216. Directory, City of Quebec, 1795, BAnQ. Only the senior positions are listed, thus Goldsworthy's name does not appear.

– Sergeant Thompson, 1 parishioner; 1 communion; 8 Protestants."[217] As in 1792, the 1798 census shows that Thompson still retained the services of a housekeeper. Interestingly, he is still referred to by his former rank in Wolfe's army.

On 27 April 1797 Robert Prescott[218] replaced Guy Carleton (Baron Dorchester) as Governor General of Canada. On 11 June 1798 Fanny gave birth to their second surviving daughter, Frances. This would be their last child; James was now in his sixty-fifth year and Fanny was in her fortieth. Still smarting over the loss of his "extra pay" ten years previously, and now with another mouth to feed, Thompson fired off a memorial to the new governor claiming his pay to be:

> ... too scanty, in feeding, cloathing [sic], and educating his young ones, in so much that, on receiving his salary every six months, he pays it away immediately in discharging his debts, and in doing of this, he has had it not in his power, for some years past, to bring one single dollar to his family, to go to market with, notwithstanding the strictest economy ... and your memorialist thinks it exceeding hard in his advanced years, to be reduced to a state of penury...[219]

This sad memorial appears to have been ignored by Governor Prescott.

On 23 April 1799, Prince EDWARD AUGUSTUS, fourth son of George III (and father of Queen Victoria) was created Duke of Kent and Strathean. In the following May, the Duke was appointed as commander-in-chief of all British forces in North America, stationed at Halifax (due to health reasons he returned home in August 1800). On 13 July 1799 Thompson's earlier application for a land grant was finally approved and he received, in joint ownership with Michel Blais (the son of his former landlord and friend), a large parcel of land in Armagh Township. The land had been surveyed on 27 August 1798 by Samuel Holland, then Surveyor General, and the land grant itself was signed by the Governor, Robert Prescott. However, the land was never used in Thompson's lifetime.[220]

Thompson was still unhappy with his government salary, and thus he lost no time sending off another memorial, this time to the newly arrived Duke of Kent, mentioning his forty-two years of faithful service during which time he had acquired "the approbation of every Commanding Engineer under whom he had served."[221] The reply from headquarters in Halifax dated 22 October 1799

---

217. The eight Protestants are likely: James; Fanny; their five children; and Fanny's aunt, Mrs. Prentice, who had moved in with the Thompson family some time after the death of her husband, Miles. This census shows that the Thompsons had taken occupancy of their house on St. Ursula Street some time before it was completed in 1800.
218. Robert Prescott was governor general from 27 April 1797 to 30 July 1799. He was replaced by Sir James Henry Craig on 24 October 1807.
219. JTC. James Thompson to Robert Prescott, Quebec, 6 August 1798.
220. *Ibid.* On Thompson's death, the land was bequeathed to his daughter, Nancy, who had married Robert Harrower, a prominent land owner in Saint-Jean-Port-Joli.
221. JTC. Memorial to HRH Edward Duke of Kent, Quebec, 4 October 1799.

bore welcome news. Backdated to 25 June 1799, Thompson's salary was to be virtually doubled to a "daily pay of seven shillings and six pence, Halifax currency, together with the several allowances of lodging and fuel."[222] Thompson received his Letter of Service on 12 November 1799, and a few days later he sent off a letter of appreciation to the Duke for his "great goodness and attention to an old servant of His Majesty...."[223]

Early in 1800 Thompson learned that in future lodging allowances would be given only to those who held a warrant, either from London or from the Commander in Chief in Canada. A letter to Lieutenant General Hunter, commanding the forces in Upper and Lower Canada, explained how this new rule would apply in Thompson's case:

> ... you may be pleased to make yourself acquainted whether the memorialist [Thompson] holds his place by a warrant from Home fixing his pay at a certain stipulated sum, or whether by an order from any former Commander in Chief, for if in the first instance, it will not be in the power of H.R.H. to serve him in any other manner than by forwarding a memorial from him, to that department from which his warrant has been issued. But if in the latter case, His Royal Highness is induced from a personal knowledge of the memorialist, and his length of faithful services together with the burden of a large family to authorise you to grant him an additional half dollar per day, so that his pay may amount to seven shillings and six pence, Currency of the Country.[224]

Surprisingly, despite being the overseer of works for Lower Canada for the past twenty-eight years, Thompson did not hold a warrant. Believing that his room allowance would be denied him, and perhaps even his new salary increase, on 28 May 1800 he fired off another letter to the Duke of Kent:

> This circumstance urged me to trouble your Royal Highness at this time humbly to request, in addition to the great good your Royal Highness has already conferred on me, that you will be graciously pleased to grant me a Warrant for the office I hold, which would not only entitle me to the emolument annexed to my office, but secure me also in my augmented salary....[225]

---

222. Major I.W. Gordon to Lieutenant General Hunter, Halifax, 22 October 1799, LAC, RG8 "C" Series, Microfilm C-2843. See also, "Letter of Service," Halifax, 22 October 1799 in Anon., *A Short Authentic Account of the Expedition against Quebec ...*, 44. (Note: £103. 14. 1 army currency was equal to £100 sterling or £111. 2. 2.67 Halifax currency. Thompson was being paid four shillings and eight pence army currency before his increase, and seven shillings and six pence Halifax currency afterwards. Therefore his increase would not have the same purchasing power if it had been continued in army currency.)
223. JTC. James Thompson to HRH Edward, Duke of Kent, Quebec, 15 November 1799.
224. Gordon to Hunter, Halifax, 22 October 1799, LAC, RG8 "C" Series, Microfilm C-2843.
225. JTC. James Thompson to Edward, Duke of Kent, Quebec, 28 May 1800.

Thompson House, St. Ursula Street. Located at the corner of St. Ursula Street and Ursulines Lane and completed in 1800, Thompson's stone house was built in the traditional "English" architectural style introduced in Lower Canada by British architects. It remained in the family until June 1957. Declared a historic monument in February 1961, today Maison historique James Thompson is a popular "bed and breakfast" in the historic part of Quebec City. (Editor's Collection)

To his great relief, Thompson was given his warrant, signed by the Duke of Kent, the receipt of which was acknowledged by Gother Mann on 7 July 1800.[226] This was extremely fortunate as a Board of Accounts had been ordered to investigate Thompson's salary over the period 25 June 1799 to 24 March 1800. The Board was fully prepared to order Thompson to pay back his salary increase if he had failed to obtain a warrant.[227]

Finally, by late 1800, Thompson's handsome new house on St. Ursula Street was essentially complete, although it would appear they had moved in some time previously. The house ended up costing him just over £251 (land acquisition, material and construction labour).[228]

Early in 1802 Thompson was ordered to report on the condition of the enclosure walls of the Jesuits' Garden, as well as providing an estimate of repair costs. When this was approved, Thompson supervised the repairs. That same year,

---

226. Gother Mann to Major Green (Military Secretary), Quebec, 7 July 1800, LAC, RG8 "C" Series, Microfilm C-2859.
227. Board of Accounts, Quebec, 12 August 1800, Colonel Mann, Royal Engineers Commandant, President, LAC, RG8 "C" Series, Microfilm C-3045.
228. About $470,000 Canadian in today's currency (equivalent purchasing power). Thompson kept a detailed account of construction costs, each entry recording material costs, the cost to move this material to the construction site, or payments to his labour force.

The "Scotch Church." Construction of the St. Andrew's Presbyterian Church, the oldest English-speaking congregation of Scottish origin in Canada, commenced in 1809 and it was dedicated the following year on its patron saint's day, 30 November 1810. James Thompson regularly attended services at St. Andrew's, "where his high stature and his venerable traits never failed to attract attention and respect." The building remains virtually unchanged but for the addition of the church vestry in 1900. (Editor's Collection)

Thompson's name was attached to a memorial sent to King George III by the Presbyterians of Quebec, petitioning for a lot of ground on which Reverend Alexander Spark and his congregation, 148 strong, could build a "decent, plain church for their public worship." Six years later, on 30 November 1808, letters patent were issued by Governor General Sir JAMES HENRY CRAIG[229] granting a lot on St. Anne's Street in Upper Town as a place for the erection of a church "for the public worship or exercise of the religion of the Church of Scotland."[230] By February 1809, £1,547 had been raised by subscription, with additional funds expected, and the building committee was ready to authorize construction. The cornerstone of the new church, officially named after the apostle Andrew but known simply in Quebec as the "Scotch Church," was laid on 23 June 1809, and we can be sure that Thompson and his family attended this important ceremony. Finally, on Sunday, 30 November 1810, Quebec's small Presbyterian congregation proudly witnessed the dedication of their new church, the culmination of years of hard work.[231] Thompson regularly attended services at St. Andrew's Church, "where his high stature and his venerable traits never failed to attract attention and respect."[232]

---

229. Craig was governor general of Canada over the period 1807 to 1811.
230. Lemoine, *Quebec Past and Present*, 404.
231. St. Andrew's Church is the oldest English-speaking congregation of Scottish origin in Canada.
232. "Décès" ("Deaths"), *La Minerve*, Montreal, 30 August 1830.

Thompson had always cherished the thought of having his sons admitted to the Royal Military Academy in Woolwich (near London). However, after lengthy correspondence with senior officers of the Ordnance Department, time had slipped by, and he eventually learned that his three eldest sons, James, William Alexander and John Gawler had by then exceeded the academy's maximum age requirement. However, George, his youngest son, still met the requirement and Thompson wrote to the former Military Secretary to Governor Haldimand, Lieutenant Colonel Robert Mathews, then living in Chelsea, to see if he could open any doors. Mathews, a close friend of Thompson who had married Mary Simpson, the daughter of his cousin Alexander "Sanders" Simpson, had considerable influence with senior officers of the Ordnance Department.

On 26 November 1803 Mathews wrote directly to John Pitt, 2nd Earl of Chatham and eldest son of William Pitt, requesting that George be considered for admission into Woolwich Academy, on behalf of an "old and worthy servant of the Crown in your Lordship's Department at Quebec," adding that it was Thompson's greatest ambition that his son "should be admitted as Cadet at Woolwich."[233] Mathews had the full support of William Twiss, by this time a full colonel with the Royal Engineers in London, and like Mathews, a close personal friend of Thompson.

On 9 December Mathews happily reported back to the Thompson family that George had been admitted to the prestigious Academy, and that all expenses in getting George to England, including the clothing and equipment he would need as a new cadet, would be handled jointly by Mathews and Twiss. After some preparatory school courses in England, George was admitted with the rank of cadet on 11 December 1804. Upon graduation, George was commissioned a lieutenant in the Royal Artillery, the first and only member of the Thompson family to obtain an officer's commission in the British army – a proud day indeed for Thompson and his family.

In 1804 Gother Mann left Quebec and he was eventually replaced as commanding engineer in Canada by Ralph Henry Bruyères, the Montreal-born son of a Huguenot who had emigrated to Canada during the Seven Years' War.[234] According to an official return dated August 1811, Thompson was still receiving a daily salary of seven shillings and six pence Halifax currency, plus an annual allowance of £20 to cover the cost of lodging.[235] In addition, he was supplied with

---

233. Robert Mathews to Lord Chatham, Horse Guards, 26 November 1803, JTC. At this time, Lord Chatham was serving as Master General of the Ordnance.
234. Bruyères was commanding engineer in Canada from 1804 to 1814. He was succeeded by Elias Walker Durnford.
235. "Return of the persons proposed to be employed during the year 1812 on the Establishment of the Engineers Department in both the Canadas together with their

"The Shop." The British Royal Military Academy at Woolwich in southeast London was established in 1741 and put the training of engineering, and later, artillery officers on a permanent footing. Its mandate was to provide an education and produce "good officers of Artillery and perfect Engineers." Thompson's youngest son, George, was admitted as a cadet in 1804 and was commissioned a first lieutenant in the Royal Artillery upon graduation in 1808. The Academy was commonly known as "The Shop" because its first building was a converted workshop of the Woolwich Arsenal. (Anne S.K. Brown Military Collection, Brown University Library)

enough firewood and candles to heat and illuminate "one room."[236] This would give Thompson an annual income of well over £160 Halifax currency, equivalent to an army lieutenant's income, which clearly placed him within the middle class of Quebec's society.[237]

But personal tragedy would strike the family in 1807. Thompson's youngest son, George, was struck by a persistent fever while serving in the 1807 Expedition to Copenhagen, "the effects of which he never overcame," and which eventually

---

allowances, Rate of pay, and the Date of their respective Appointments," Quebec, August 1811, LAC, RG8 "C" Series, Microfilm C-3839. The word "proposed" in this document clearly shows that Thompson's position was always tenuous.
236. This would be the yearly entitlement, i.e. the bulk amount of firewood and candles he would be entitled to. Other positions, such as assistant clerk of works, would receive enough firewood and candles for "½ Room."
237. In terms of equivalent purchasing power (retail price index calculations), this would equate to about $90,000 Canadian in 2007.

developed into a fatal lung condition.[238] While at Gibraltar in 1816, George managed an exchange to Montreal in hopes that a change to a more familiar location would return his health. Sadly, on 12 February 1817, the young artillery subaltern passed away – he was twenty-seven years of age.

Two of his brothers, William and John, rushed to Montreal to attend his funeral, but a severe winter storm delayed their arrival. George was buried in Montreal without a family member present, but he was given a proper burial with all military honours by his fellow officers. Thompson's oldest son, James Jr., heartbroken over the loss of his younger brother, but more concerned with how his aging parents would take the devastating news, wrote the following entry in his diary:

> … thus were the fondest hopes of a parent, for the advancement in life of a much beloved son, blighted as it were in the bud: and the anxious solicitude of many previous years dashed to the ground.… I may say that this is the only occasion on which I had observed the proofs of despondency visible on the features of my venerable father. He had lived to experience many transitions of fate, but his great strength of mind, aided by religious feeling, enabled him to surmount each resuscitade [*sic*] with apparent calmness. His loss was a severe trial of his fortitude, and it was a long time before he again resumed his wonted cheerfulness, a frame of feeling for which he was much celebrated. It is not in my recollection that he ever mentioned George's name afterwards.[239]

But time rolled on. In 1816 yet another new commanding engineer arrived to replace Ralph Bruyères, who had died in 1814 – ELIAS WALKER DURNFORD.[240] In that same year, Thompson moved into a new office building which had been added to the Royal Engineers Yard and Complex, located in and near the gorge of the St. Louis Bastion.[241]

In 1818 Thompson was informed that he could continue on as the overseer of military works at Quebec though his advanced age would suggest that by this time the position was now looked upon as an honorary appointment, one

---

238. JTC.
239. *Ibid*.
240. Durnford was commanding engineer in Canada from 1816 to 1831. His major accomplishment was the design and construction of Quebec's permanent citadel, built over the period 1819–32. Durnford would be Thompson's last commanding engineer.
241. The Royal Engineers Yard, with its offices, workshops, storehouses, forge and barracks, was located in and adjacent to the gorge of the St. Louis Bastion. This yard served the engineers as well as the sappers and miners. The main office building, facing St. Louis Street, had separate offices for the commandant, Royal Engineers, the adjutant, the clerk of works, the senior clerk, and the foreman, as well as a large drawing office. The office for the overseer of works, along with the officer commanding the District Office, was located in a small, separate office building in this yard. Today the site is occupied by Quebec's prestigious Garrison Club, founded in 1879 by Canadian militia officers.

St. Louis Street, 1830. Each morning James Thompson would have left his house on St. Ursula Street (rue Sainte-Ursule) and turned right onto this street to walk to work. To the left of the St. Louis Gate in the distance we see the tall trees marking the entrance to Judge Jonathan Sewell's mansion. The gracious house set back from the street on the right was originally constructed for the United Empire Loyalist Thomas Aston Coffin, a politically significant figure in the "Château Clique" around Governor Guy Carleton, Lord Dorchester. The garrison's engineering offices, where Thompson worked in his later years, were located adjacent to the St. Louis Gate. Watercolour by James Pattison Cockburn. (LAC C-10655).

which recognized his fifty-eight years of continuous service. He certainly wasn't as active around the garrison and the surrounding countryside as he was in former years but the following incident shows that Thompson could still be of considerable service to the government.

In 1818 Stephen van Rensselaer, the former lieutenant governor of New York State, obtained permission from Governor General Sir JOHN COAPE SHERBROOKE[242] for the remains of American Revolutionary War general Richard Montgomery to be moved from Quebec to New York.[243] Some years previously, Thompson had taken the precaution to mark the grave when he had learned that the old powder magazine located in the gorge of the St. Louis Bastion was

---

242. Sherbrooke was governor general of Canada from 12 July 1816 to 29 July 1818.
243. Montgomery had fallen at Quebec on 31 December 1775.

to be demolished and replaced by barracks, although he was quick to add the real reason: "not so much perhaps on *his* account, as from the interest I felt in it on *another* score."[244] Thompson was referring, of course, to the grave of his first wife, which he had marked with a small cut stone inserted into the pavement within the barrack square. It would be this marker which helped Thompson to locate Montgomery's grave.

On 16 June, with Chief Justice JONATHAN SEWELL and several officers of the garrison in attendance, Thompson pointed to the exact spot where the workmen should dig. Montgomery's skeleton was found complete, and when removed, a musket ball fell out from the skull.

On 8 July General Montgomery's remains were interred next to his monument in St. Paul's Chapel in New York City. Thompson was asked to give an affidavit concerning the facts of Montgomery's death in order to satisfy the surviving relatives that the remains were truly those of the late general. As can be seen in the narrative dated 19 June 1818 below, Thompson couldn't resist telling the story of the general's sword:

> 19 June 1818 – I, James Thompson, of Quebec ... do testify and declare – that I served in the capacity of an Assistant Engineer during the siege of this city, invested during the years 1775 and 1776 by the American forces under the command of the late Major General Richard Montgomery. That in an attack made by the American troops ... in the night of the 31st December 1775, on a British post at the southernmost extremity of the city near Près-de-Ville, the General received a mortal wound, and with him were killed his two Aides-de-Camp, McPherson and Cheeseman, who were found in the morning of the 1st January 1776 almost covered with snow. That Mrs. Prentice who kept an Hotel at Quebec, and with whom General Montgomery had previously boarded was brought to view the body after it was placed in the Guard Room, and which she recognized by a particular mark which he had on the side of his head to be the general's ... that in the night of the 4th January, it was interred six feet in front of the gate, within a wall that surrounded a powder magazine near the ramparts bounding on St. Lewis [*sic*] Gate. That the funeral service was performed at the grave by the Reverend Mr. De Montmolin, then Chaplain of the garrison. That his two Aides-de-Camp were buried in their clothes without any coffins, and that no person was buried within twenty-five feet of the General. That I am positive and can testify and declare, that the coffin of the late General Montgomery taken up on the morning of the 16th of the present month of June, 1818, is the identical coffin deposited by me on the day of his burial, and that the present coffin contains the remains of the late General. I do further testify and declare that subsequent to the finding of General Montgomery's body, I wore his sword, being lighter than my own, and on going to the Seminary, where the American officers were lodged, they recognized the sword, which affected

---

244. JTC – Anecdote 29. Emphasis is Thompson's.

them so much, that numbers of them wept, in consequence of which I have never worn the sword since. Given under my hand, at the city of Quebec, James Thompson.[245]

Thompson was the consummate story-teller, always quick to conjure up his fascinating (and sometimes hilarious) stories about his former exploits with Fraser's Highlanders, in particular those involving his beloved General Wolfe, who had become an iconic figure. While undoubtedly respected by his many friends and colleagues, it does not seem that Thompson attracted much public notice over much of his life. However, the following incident with the Duke of Richmond shows that by 1818 the old veteran had achieved a measure of celebrity in Quebec City. With the attention shown to him by the Duke of Richmond, and later by Lord and Lady Dalhousie, Thompson's stature as a veteran of Wolfe's army would only grow and mature like a vintage wine.

On 30 July 1818 CHARLES LENNOX, Duke of Richmond, arrived to take up his duties as Governor General of Canada. Shortly after his arrival in Quebec, the Duke attended a parade of the troops on the Esplanade and, spotting Thompson in the crowd, walked over and asked him a few questions about Fraser's Highlanders. Thompson handled these questions with his usual aplomb, a large crowd gathering to see and hear the old Highlander, leaving him to quip, "I assure you, I felt within myself that it was no small matter to become acquainted with me!" Thompson added, "while I yet stood with my hat in my hand, his Grace walked away saying that he was glad to see me looking so well, and he wished me 'good morning' although it was not far from six in the evening!"[246]

During that same year, another census was held in Quebec, this one indexed, but only showing the head of household. It reads: "Ste. Ursule Street, No. 24, Thompson, James – Engineer"[247]

Interestingly, no longer is he "Sergeant Thompson," but rather, "James Thompson, Engineer." Likely, this was the answer he gave when asked for his occupation by the enumerator, all part of his desire to climb to a higher social position than would normally be attached to a sergeant.

The Duke of Richmond's tenure as governor would be short-lived. On 28 June 1819, during a tour of the Canadas, he was bitten by a supposedly tame

---

245. Affidavit, James Thompson, 19 June 1818, quoted in Henry B. Dawson, *The Historical Magazine, Notes & Queries, concerning the Antiquities, History & Biography of America*, vol II, 3rd Series (Morrisania, N.Y., 1873), 295-6.
246. JTC – Anecdote 31. It would appear that this little quip became an "inside" joke within the family. It would be fondly remembered, and used, by James Jr. in 1828 when Lord Dalhousie firmly shook his hand in front of Quebec's military and civilian elite. This incident will be related further on in this monograph.
247. Joseph Signaÿ, *Recensement de la ville de Québec en 1818, Cahiers d'Histoire #29* (Quebec, 1976).

fox recently purchased by a member of his staff for his amusement.[248] He died of rabies on 28 August 1819, a few miles from Richmond in Upper Canada. His remains were brought back to Quebec and interred with great pomp and ceremony in the Anglican Cathedral.

He was replaced as Governor General by GEORGE RAMSAY, the 9th Earl of Dalhousie.[249] Dalhousie's frequent journeys across Canada were the hallmark of his approach to governing and, during his twelve-year tenure, he sponsored a number of artists who accompanied him on his official visits to the four provinces that formed British North America at that time. One of these artists was Captain JOHN CRAWFORD YOUNG, a grenadier captain in the 79th Regiment (Cameron Highlanders), one of four aides de camp retained by Dalhousie. It appears that Captain Young developed a close affinity with Thompson, the former grenadier sergeant with Fraser's Highlanders. During his posting to Canada, Young would execute at least forty landscape and genre paintings for Dalhousie, all "recommended by His Excellency … as a good subject for a sketch."[250]

Since 1821, Dalhousie had revelled in the company of old Thompson, then approaching ninety years of age. While Thompson was certainly in his twilight years, he was still capable of telling a good story and he was often invited to dine with Dalhousie at the "Castle,"[251] of which the following invitation is typical:

> Castle of Saint Louis, Tuesday, December 1827 – My Dear Sir. If the weather is not too severe, and our hours not too late for you, will you do me the favor to dine with me on Saturday next, dinner on Table at six. I hope to see your sons with you. Your's with great respect and regard. Dalhousie.[252]

Dalhousie kept a private diary and Thompson's name appears in a number of places:

> 13 April 1823 – Sunday. Yesterday, old Thompson in the Engineers' Office dined with me; I have mentioned him repeatedly before[253] as one of the only remaining companions of Wolfe on the plains of Abraham. He was then a sergeant in Fraser's Highlanders… It is astonishing with how much accuracy he speaks of the most trifling circumstances, and names not only officers in high rank, but of all ranks … who did their deeds of valour in some conspicuous instance. Sir

---

248. Henry J. Morgan, *Sketches of Celebrated Canadians and Persons Connected with Canada…* (Quebec, 1862), 242.
249. Dalhousie spent twelve years in Canada as a colonial administrator.
250. Marie Elwood, "Studies in Documents: the Discovery and Repatriation of the Lord Dalhousie Collection," *Archivaria* 24 (Summer 1987), 109.
251. Castle of St. Louis, the governor general's residence in Quebec.
252. JTC.
253. This suggests that Thompson had been mentioned in earlier diary entries. However, many pages of Dalhousie's private journal are in poor condition and the editors have been unable to locate these earlier entries.

"I've lost my best friend!" So lamented a ninety-six-year-old James Thompson when his patron and benefactor, George Ramsay, 9th Earl of Dalhousie (1770–1838), the governor-in-chief of British North America, left Quebec in 1828 to return to Britain. Initially appointed lieutenant governor of Nova Scotia, where he championed improved methods of farming and road-building, Dalhousie also helped found the university in Halifax that bears his name. He subsequently became governor-in-chief of British North America in November 1819 after the sudden death of the Duke of Richmond. Enchanted and impressed by Thompson's stories and excellent memory, Dalhousie invited "the gallant old Highlander" to dine at the Governor's palace on many occasions. (Anne S. K. Brown Military Collection, Brown University Library)

Francis Burton[254] pumped the whole story out of him but never put him out nor tired him. There is a bust of Wolfe in this house and a strong likeness had been observed in it to Sir George Beckwith.[255] When asked if he saw the likeness in Sir George to General Wolfe he paused awhile, "No I don't think so – I never yet saw a man like him – he was a noble soldier, and always carried his fusee slung upon him." This last sentence closed everything he said about Wolfe personally, he seemed never to tire of repeating this particular feature in his character – the enthusiasm of the old man was delightful. He is now in his 93rd year. He played several games at Backgammon last night with Lady Dalhousie and beat her. It is the usual pastime of his evenings and he played quick and sharp, and even without the aid of spectacles.[256]

Dalhousie also had this to say about the backgammon games:

After these dinners, it was delightful to see the pleasure he took in playing backgammon with Lady Dalhousie and still more so to witness the glean of the old man if he beat her, as was not infrequently the case ... he could detect the back [backgammon] mistake in an instant, so sharp and quick was he at that advanced age.[257]

By early 1821, Thompson's house had fallen into a dangerous state of disrepair. In recognition of his years of faithful service, and "as a mark of respect to one of the only surviving companions in arms of the immortal Wolfe," Dalhousie ordered Colonel Durnford, commanding engineer, to undertake certain "repairs to the house he now occupies in Quebec, and which appears to His Lordship in a dangerous state."[258]

But by 1825 Thompson was finding it increasingly difficult to make the trek to and from the Royal Engineers offices on St. Louis Street. Then ninety-two years of age, the old veteran could be seen each morning "with bent frame supported only by his long staff, for he disdained their assistance, slowly pacing from

---

254. Governor of Lower Canada.
255. Sir George Beckwith (1753–1823) distinguished himself as a regimental officer in the American Revolutionary War and served subsequently in high administration posts and in numerous successful military operations in the West Indies during the French Revolutionary and Napoleonic wars. He was made a K.B. for his capture of Martinique in 1809 and attained the full rank of general in 1814. He commanded the forces in Ireland, 1816–20. He died in London on 20 March 1823.
256. George Ramsay, 9th Earl of Dalhousie Fonds, LAC, MG24-A12, Microfilm A-536. For an edited version, see also Whitelaw, *Dalhousie Journals*.
257. James Thompson Jr. to Colonel John Ramsay, Quebec, 8 September 1828, NAS, GD45/3/422, folios 490–91. John Ramsay was aide de camp (and brother) to George Ramsay, Earl of Dalhousie.
258. H.C. Darling to Lieutenant Colonel Durnford, Quebec, 25 [unreadable] 1821. James T. Harrower Papers, CWM.

St. Louis Gate, 1829. This detail of Image 7 on page 107 (see "A Colour Album") shows the interior façade of the St. Louis Gate (centre) and the Royal Engineers main office building (left), facing onto St. Louis Street. The main office building had separate offices for the Commandant, Royal Engineers, and his direct supporting staff (adjutant, clerk of works, senior clerk, etc.) as well as a large draughting office. The Royal Engineers yard and complex was located in the rear of this building. Thompson had a smaller office building in this complex, known as the Overseer of Works Building, which he shared with the officer commanding the district office, although they had separate offices. Watercolour by James Pattison Cockburn. (Royal Ontario Museum 942.48.85)

his house to his office by half past nine every morning, and as regularly on the Sabbath did he attend the services of his God in the Presbyterian Church."[259]

Lord Dalhousie had tried to get Thompson to retire, but the offer was politely rejected as the old Highlander preferred to continue his duties while his strength remained:

> Lord Dalhousie, thinking him fully entitled at this late period to an honourable retirement, with characteristic benevolence, signified his disposition to interest himself with His Majesty's Government to procure Mr. Thompson a pension for the remainder of his days. The old gentleman politely acknowledged his sense of His Lordship's kindness, but preferred the continuance of his duties while strength remained sufficient to attend his office.[260]

---

259. James Thompson Jr. to Colonel John Ramsay, Quebec, 8 September 1828, NAS, GD45/3/422, folios 490–91.
260. Alfred Hawkins, *Picture of Quebec: with Historical Recollections* (Quebec, 1834), 474 (Note 18).

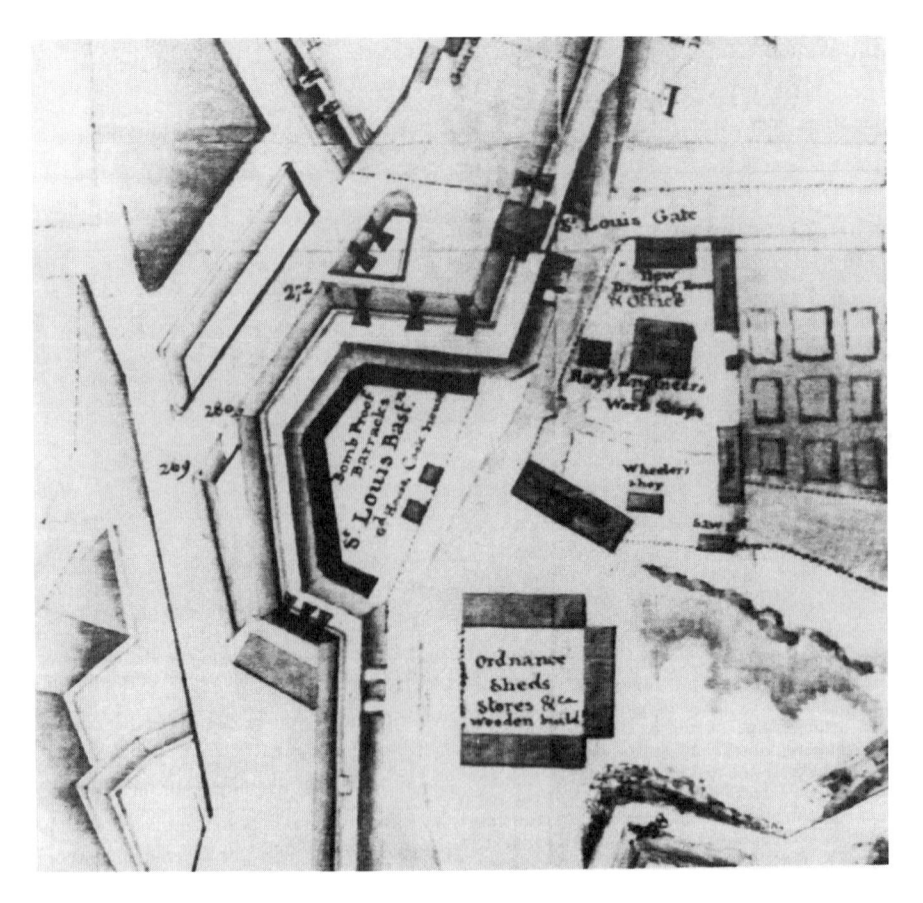

Royal Engineers Yard, 1816. The Royal Engineers yard and the inner gorge of the St. Louis Bastion formed a military complex that was gradually enlarged during the 1820s and '30s to facilitate the final construction of the Citadel. Consisting of office buildings, workshops, forge, storehouses, as well as the large "splinter proof" barracks on the left, used by the sappers and miners. Previously, the gorge contained a powder magazine as well as a small Protestant burial ground. When Thompson's first wife died, she was buried here with the powder magazine as a visual reference. When he learned that the powder magazine was to be demolished and replaced by barracks, Thompson took the precaution to mark the grave with a small cut stone, inserted into the pavement within the barrack square. It would be this marker which helped Thompson locate General Richard Montgomery's grave in 1818. Today, this site is occupied by the Garrison Club, founded in 1879 by Canadian militia officers. (LAC, National Map Collection, H2/340/Quebec/1816)

Thompson must have known that it was time to step down and take his well-deserved retirement, but the exact date and circumstance of his official retirement, if he had one, are not known. However, the following letter suggests that he retired sometime in 1825: "Since 1825 he has been obliged to give up his desk and to retire … a privilege which had been at his option for many years, but which as long as he could walk from his house to his office he would never hear of accepting."[261]

When he did retire, his duties (which must have been quite minimal by this time) were temporarily taken over by the clerk of works, William Morrison.[262] Interestingly, and perhaps with considerable tongue-in-cheek, Thompson privately gave the reason for his "early" retirement as an "infirmity, contracted during the fatigues of the American War in 1775...."[263]

The following additional diary entries by Lord Dalhousie are of interest:

> 3 December 1826, Sunday – On 30th St. Andrew's Day was kept by both the Scotch regiments in garrison. I dined with the 79th [Regiment] and never in my life have I seen a more jovial happy party. Colonel Douglas in the Chair, who only left it when he could sit no longer on it. Old Thompson, the companion of Wolfe of the Plains of Abraham, dined there, now 94 years of age; I was requested to propose his health, and did so with some short compliment to him as a soldier, a Highlander, a venerable father in the midst of us boys in comparison. There was not a man in the room who was born when he wore his kilt at the conquest of Canada. We gave him three roaring cheers, and the old Gentleman returned his thanks very well. Soon after, 3 capital Pipers entered, playing the gathering of the Clans. The old man seemed to be quite delighted. When he left the room, two of the officers with all the Pipers walked him safely to his own house.

> 7 January 1827, Sunday – Old Thompson dined with me today, with two of his sons.... Of course the conversation was all upon Wolfe, and the same clear recollection of the old man told his stories in the very same words he has always told them so very clear that I sat down before I went to bed to write one or two of his long ones. He said he felt now that he was growing frail, that on 13th March he would be 94 years complete. I don't exactly remember how this tallies with his account of himself in former years but I see no change in him in these 7 years past. He told several anecdotes suggested on the moment by the naming of ships, Regiments and individuals. He particularly spoke of the Southampton and Lowestoff frigates but forgetting others. I sent for Jeffries' [Thomas Jeffreys'] history of the siege of Quebec and it brought to his mind the Diana [frigate] and several more of which he spoke with the same readiness and perfect recollection. He said that General Wolfe never addressed a man whom he did not know by name, in any other way than "Brother soldier," and the Highlanders never called him by any name but "The red [haired] Corporal" in Gaelic [Cennaire Ruandaidh]. He told us a very long story of one Duncan

---

261. James Thompson Jr. to Colonel John Ramsay, Quebec, 8 September 1828, NAS, GD45/3/422, folios 490–91.
262. *The Quebec Almanac* for the years 1830 and 1831 shows that the position of overseer of works was vacant. It was finally filled in 1832 by Edward Erson.
263. "Concerning the Journal of James Thompson, 1758–1830," LHSQ, *Transactions*, New Series, No. 22 (1898).

McPhie – whom he seemed to speak of with great regard.... The old man drank his wine freely, played as usual some hits at backgammon with Lady D., not using spectacles, and walked away to his home at half past 10 PM. I do think him one of the most remarkable instances of long life I ever met with.[264]

On 21 March 1827, Lord Dalhousie, as a special mark of respect, appointed Thompson's son, John Gawler, as a Judge for the District of Gaspé:

My Dear Sir, – I gave you no answer to your last letter and walk down to the Castle; and it, therefore, gives me pleasure to do, without any solicitation, that which I hope will assure you of my wish to testify my respect for you and yours. I have this moment named your son to be Judge in Gaspé, an important and respectable station in society, and which must grow more in consequence as society increases and enlarges in that fine district of Canada.

Yours most truly, DALHOUSIE.[265]

In August 1827 the *Quebec Gazette*[266] published an article announcing that Lord Dalhousie had proposed to erect a joint memorial to Generals James Wolfe and Louis-Joseph de Montcalm, commemorating their deaths on the Plains of Abraham in 1759.[267] Designed by Captain John Crawford Young, one of Dalhousie's aides-de-camp, it was to be erected in a prominent position near the Château Saint-Louis overlooking the river. While it eventually became known as the Wolfe–Montcalm monument, Dalhousie always considered it as "Wolfe's monument." Bearing the names of the two generals, it would feature an obelisk rising 20 feet. Showing good feeling as well as good taste, both French and English were eschewed in favour of Latin in the two inscriptions: the longer of these is a description of the monument's genesis; the shorter a tribute to the two generals:

---

264. George Ramsay, 9th Earl of Dalhousie Fonds, LAC, MG 24-A12, Microfilm A-536. For an edited version, see Whitelaw, *Dalhousie Journals*.
265. Dalhousie to James Thompson, Quebec, 21 March 1827, quoted in *A Short Authentic Account...*, 45.
266. The *Quebec Gazette*, founded by William Brown and Thomas Gilmore, began publication on 21 June 1764, the earliest newspaper in the city. Bilingual from the beginning, it merged with the *Chronicle* to become the *Chronicle and Quebec Gazette* on 1 May 1923.
267. Up to this time, the only memorial to General Wolfe *in Quebec City* was a large wood statue on the corner of St. John and Palace Streets, which Thompson helped the sculptors to execute. Outside the city proper was the large stone which the army rolled to mark the spot where Wolfe died on the Plains of Abraham, uninscribed and later forgotten. It was replaced by another stone in 1789, installed on the spot where Wolfe was believed to have died (as no trace of the original stone could be found). By 1832 this second stone had been ruined by vandals, and it was replaced by a column erected by Lord Aylmer, then governor general (pieces of the former rock were left under the foundation). This third memorial was reproduced (with the same decorative helmet) in 1913 by the National Battlefields Commission.

"A Common Memorial." Designed by Captain John Crawford Young, one of Dalhousie's aides de camp, the original Wolfe–Montcalm memorial, a 20-foot obelisk, was erected in a prominent position near the Château Saint-Louis overlooking the river. Its Latin inscription was a tribute to the two generals who both died from their battle wounds: *"Their courage gave them a common death/history a common fame/posterity a common memorial."* As the oldest living survivor of Wolfe's army, James Thompson was given the honour of helping Lord Dalhousie lay the foundation stone on 15 November 1827. In April 2010 the entire monument, which stands next to the present day Château Frontenac Hotel, was dismantled and rebuilt by Parks Canada, many of the crumbling stones replaced by new ones. (Anne S.K. Brown Military Collection, Brown University Library)

> Mortem Virtus Communem
> Famam Historia
> Monumentum Posteritas Dedit.[268]

A public subscription was organized, and the money was raised in record time, though to Dalhousie's chagrin there was little interest shown by Canadians and he was forced to contribute a large sum of money to complete the subscription.

The foundation stone was laid on 15 November 1827 with considerable ceremony. With the streets lined with troops, the Grand Lodge of Masons walked in majestic procession and full masonic costume towards the Château, followed by Lady Dalhousie and her ladies-in-waiting. They in turn were followed by Lord Dalhousie accompanied by the Lord Bishop of Quebec and the Chief Justice, all attended by the officers of the garrison and the governor's staff.

But the most interesting person in attendance was none other than James Thompson. One of the last known living survivors of the battle on the Plains of Abraham in Canada, Thompson had been given the honour of helping Lord Dalhousie lay the foundation stone. The old Highlander, then in his ninety-fourth year, struggled to get to the ceremony, as by this time his mobility had become severely impaired – friends and family had been urging him for some time to use a "truss" so that he could "walk out."[269] The stone, laid with full Masonic honours, was first tried by Claude Dénéchau, the Right Worshipful Grand Master of the Provincial Grand Lodge of Quebec and Three Rivers. Next, the mallet was handed to Brother Thompson, the oldest member of the Craft present, with Lord Dalhousie stating: "Mr. Thompson, we honour you here as the companion-in-arms and a venerable living witness of the fall of Wolfe, do us the favour to bear witness on this occasion, by the Mallet in your hand."[270]

Supported by the arm of his companion-in-arms, Captain Young, Thompson gave the traditional "three mystic strokes" with the mallet on the stone. The troops then fired a *feu de joie*, the crowd gave three hearty British cheers and the ceremony was over.

For some time now, confidence in Lord Dalhousie's administration had been steadily waning at the Colonial Office in London and his time in Canada was nearing an end. In 1827, likely through his friends in the Admiralty, Dalhousie was appointed commander-in-chief of the army in India and advised to set out for his new command as soon as possible.

In February 1828 John Robertson, formerly a soldier in Fraser's Highlanders,

---

268. Translation: *Their courage gave them a common death, history a common fame, posterity a common memorial.*
269. John Gawler Thompson to Fanny Thompson, Douglass Town, 22 August 1828, NAS, GD45/3/422, folio 498.
270. Quoted in Gale, *Historic Tales*, 112.

died at the age of ninety-seven years in the parish of St. Roch. With his death, a local newspaper reported, "We believe that Mr. James Thompson is now the sole survivor of that Army remaining in this Province."[271]

On 16 April 1828 Thompson's recollections of his experiences with Fraser's Highlanders reached a much wider audience when his account of Sergeant Allan Cameron's narrow escape during the retreat near Montmorency Falls in 1759 dominated a page of a local newspaper, the *Star and Commercial Advertiser*, under the headline "Anecdotes of Wolfe's Army."[272] This was the first of a series of four articles in this newspaper. While attributed only to "a companion in arms on that occasion," it was clearly the words of James Thompson.[273] The next article covered the 1758 landing at Louisbourg with the following explanation added by the newspaper's editor:

> We publish in today's paper, an account of the landing of Wolfe's Army at Louisburg, which will be read we are sure with interest, by all our Subscribers. How superior are the beauties of the plain unadorned narrative of one who had been an actor in the scenes which he describes, to the meretricious ornaments of a false Rhetoric! We hope to have it in our power to enrich our Columns with more papers like this from the same venerable hand.[274]

On 1 June 1828 Thompson prepared his Last Will and Testament, leaving his house, furniture and moveables to his beloved Fanny, adding that it was his wish that their home on St. Ursula Street "may not go out of my family."[275] He bequeathed his portion of the vacant land in Armagh Township to his daughter, Nancy, who had married Robert Harrower and was living in nearby Saint-Jean-Port-Joli. One of the witnesses to his will was William Morrison, the clerk of the works for the Royal Engineers who had taken over Thompson's duties. By his son's account, Thompson had long prepared himself for death, "without any of the terrors which he had experienced on the battlefield"; in fact, he welcomed death "as one of mercy and relief from his long and weary pilgrimage."[276]

---

271. "Death of a Veteran of Wolfe's Army," *Star and Commercial Advertiser*, 20 February 1828.
272. "Anecdotes of Wolfe's Army," *Star and Commercial Advertiser*, 10 May 1828. Other articles were dated 10 May, 28 June, and 28 July 1828.
273. The 10 May 1828 article published in the *Star and Commercial Advertiser* was reprinted by LHSQ, Centenary Volume: 1824–1924, *Transactions*, New Series, No. 30 (1924), with the following note added by Lord Dalhousie: "This is the style, phrase, and very words of old Thompson of Quebec now in his 90th year; he was a sergeant in Fraser's Highlanders under Wolfe, and has recounted to me many such stories, with astonishing recollection and accuracy of detail – 'D'".
274. "Anecdotes of Wolfe's Army," *Star and Commercial Advertiser*, 10 May 1828.
275. James Thompson, "Last Will and Testament." James T. Harrower Papers, CWM.
276. James Thompson Jr. to Colonel John Ramsay, Quebec, 8 September 1828, NAS, GD45/3/422, folios 490–91.

During 1828 two Americans (a historian named Ford and a painter named Gibson) visited Quebec expressly to talk to Thompson and obtain information regarding the 1775 American attack on Quebec and the death of General Montgomery. James Thompson Jr. noted that during the visit "Mr. Gibson begged to be allowed to take my father's portrait, for the purpose of being appended to an historical work then in a state of progress."[277]

On 10 June 1828 James Jr. was relieved of all duties and placed on the army's half-pay list (effective 25 July). At that time he was the assistant commissary general stationed at Cedars, Quebec, having worked in the commissariat department[278] since he was thirteen years old.[279] This was perhaps the first sign of a changing relationship between the Thompson family and the military, now that Dalhousie was on the way out. While unfortunate for the Thompson family, it was quite fortunate in other respects as James Jr. now found himself "so much at leisure"[280] and in a position to start recording his father's oral stories, his "anecdotes of Wolfe's army." As a result, James Jr. became the first editor of his father's memoirs.

On the morning of 20 August 1828 Colonel John Ramsay, Lord Dalhousie's brother and aide de camp, dropped by Thompson's house with a letter from Lord Dalhousie. Apparently an American general named Lewis was in town and had asked Dalhousie if he could pay his respects to Thompson and talk to him about General Richard Montgomery. As soon as he arrived, Colonel Ramsay was ushered upstairs to talk to James Jr., so as not to disturb old Thompson, who was resting "below stairs and very unwell from the loss of his hearing."[281] (By this time, Thompson was unable to make it up the narrow staircase to his bedroom and was confined to his dining room.)

When Colonel Ramsay learned that Thompson was too weak to "undergo the recital of the particulars solicited by General Lewis," he quickly departed but left Dalhousie's letter. When this letter was later read back to Thompson, he told James Jr. to immediately write a note back to Colonel Ramsay, telling him that Dalhousie's "highly favored" request had revived him, and that he would

---

277. Dawson, *The Historical Magazine*, 299. A thorough search has failed to uncover either the portrait or the historical work.
278. The Commissariat Department accompanied the army on all its movements, with responsibility for rations, transportation and, particularly in Canada, barracks. In the British army, the Commissariat was the military arm of the Treasury Board and its officers held a War Office commission. In 1869 officers were transferred to the new "Control Department," which is 1888 became the Army Service Corps.
279. Ever the dutiful son, he turned down other offers of employment, likely instigated by Dalhousie, to remain close to his aging parents.
280. JTC.
281. *Ibid.*, Anecdote 37.

be happy to "receive the honor of General Lewis' visit about noon tomorrow, or the following day." James Jr. took this opportunity to give Colonel Ramsay the completed statement of Thompson's services that had been requested by the Board of Ordnance, "to which he has affixed his signature."[282]

Thompson's statement of his services was a lengthy, rambling document which finally ended with a heart-rending request that the Board "continue to me the emoluments of a situation," the formal mid-19th century manner of asking for a pension:

> I will only further state, in a brief manner, that I have ever had a great degree of confidence placed in me by my superiors in office, and that I have had the good fortune to render that satisfaction which is one of the greatest consolations to me in the fast declining stage of a career, which, through the interposition of Providential agency has already been extended to the *ninety sixth year!* The books and other official documents of the Royal Engineer Department will bear testimony, not only to the extent of the duties I have performed, but also to the protracted period to which I continued to discharge them; and if the infirmities which are peculiar to extreme-age, now constrain me to desist from my wanted exertions, I cherish a confidence that the Respective Officers will, from their knowledge of further circumstances which I have not touched upon in this place, make such a communication in my behalf to the Honourable The Master-General and Board of Ordnance, as will induce that Honourable Board to continue to me the emoluments of a situation which has received the best energies of a long life almost exclusively devoted to its interests, and the enjoyment of which emoluments, in the usual course of nature, cannot be viewed as attaching a burden upon the Public, which it might not reasonably bear for a short space of time.[283]

Ever the practical Scotsman, Thompson concluded his memorandum with a reminder that any burden on the public purse would only last for a short period of time.

Meanwhile the erection of the Wolfe–Montcalm monument was progressing rapidly, every effort being expended by both military and civilian workers to ensure its completion prior to Dalhousie's departure from Canada. It was completed on 8 September 1828, one day before he was scheduled to leave, and on that same day James Jr. sent a few papers to Colonel Ramsay as a reminder to Lord Dalhousie "on subjects of a nature for which a lively interest has been shewn by His Lordship," adding that the papers "may, at a leisure moment, perhaps afford some amusement, if not pleasurable feeling."[284]

---

282. *Ibid.*
283. *Ibid.*, Anecdote 38, "Memorandum of the most arduous Services performed by James Thompson, Overseer of Works, since his joining the Engineer Department at Quebec in the Year 1761," 31 July 1828.
284. James Thompson Jr., to Colonel John Ramsay, Quebec, 8 September 1828. NAS,

On 8 September 1828 Lord Dalhousie presided at a ceremony to place the top stone on his so-called "Wolfe's Monument," only one day before his departure from Canada. Thompson was too ill to attend the ceremony, or in the words of James Jr., he was "much too enfeebled by age."[285]

On the morning of his departure, Dalhousie held a levee at the Castle of St. Louis for invited officers and guests, including James Thompson, Jr., resplendent in the uniform of a senior officer of the commissariat corps.[286] While James was making his obligatory reception-line bow, Dalhousie stepped forward and firmly took his hand, saying: "I beg Mr. Thompson that you will present my best compliments to your good father, and tell him that it was my intention to have called upon him, but in his present weak state, I think that would be too much for him to bear."[287]

James Jr. expressed his father's regret in not being able to attend the reception in person, but for James Jr., being singled out by a representative of the King on so conspicuous an occasion "was a moment of great honour and a species of pride stole across my feelings, verifying as it were the quaint saying of my father 'that it was no small matter to become acquainted with me.'"[288]

On the day of Dalhousie's departure, Captain Young was given the unhappy task of telling Thompson that his friend had been recalled back to England. Sitting quietly with the old man in his garden, Young broke the bad news. Thompson was devastated, crying out repeatedly, "So, I've lost my best friend, Dalhousie!" At dinner that night Thompson raised a glass of wine to the "Health and Prosperity of His Lordship." Using the same drink, "he being too unwell and weak to bear a second …," he raised his glass again to the "Health and Happiness of Her Ladyship." Over dinner, Captain Young asked if he could be allowed to take Thompson's portrait the next day, but secretly the family knew that the request was "at the instance of His Lordship, and in the intention that it should be sent after him to England."[289]

GD45/3/422, folios 490–91. The package included a few copies of his father's "Anecdotes of Wolfe's army"; a letter from Judge John Gawler Thompson to his mother, Fanny Thompson, dated 22 August 1828; as well as a covering letter from James Jr.

285. JTC – Anecdote 35.
286. While placed on the half-pay list, he was still entitled to wear his uniform and carry his former title at sanctioned social events.
287. JTC – Anecdote 35.
288. *Ibid*.
289. *Ibid*. The location of Young's pen and ink portrait sketch of James Thompson is unknown. Presumably it was sent back to Scotland with other items belonging to Lord Dalhousie. It is not part of Young's "American Portfolio No. 1" acquired by the National Gallery of Canada in 1985, nor has it ever been seen by Dalhousie's descendants in Scotland. However, the editors believe that the portrait of James Thompson featured elsewhere in this book is the sketch executed by Young on 9 September 1828. While

While Thompson missed the official ceremony to place the final stone atop the Wolfe–Montcalm Monument, he was compelled to see the monument to his beloved Wolfe one last time. On 21 September 1828, assisted by James Jr., he slowly walked from his house to the monument. His son recorded that "his enfeebled state made it a serious undertaking, he having been obliged to rest himself frequently, by sitting on the steps of street doors. So also was he very much exhausted on his return home."[290] Sadly, it would be the last time Thompson would ever leave his house.

Early in 1829 Thompson received a letter from the Secretary of the Board of Ordnance in London, advising him that he had been granted an "allowance of superannuation" (in effect, a pension) of £188 per annum, effective 1 January 1829.[291] It would appear that his "best friend," Dalhousie, had not forgotten him and had pulled the necessary strings. For some reason, perhaps health issues, Thompson took some time before he officially acknowledged this letter, but eventually he dispatched a letter to the Board offering his thanks "for the liberality that has been exercised in my behalf."[292]

Thompson's health continued to deteriorate and by late July 1830, knowing the end was near, the family sent for William Thompson, then stationed with the Commissariat Department in Kingston, Upper Canada. William rushed to his dying father's side "and was in close attendance upon the wants of our common parent, and experienced the high gratification that his attentions were duly appreciated, even unto his last hour."[293]

On 25 August 1830 James Thompson quietly passed away in the family home on St. Ursula Street. He was in his ninety-eighth year. His death entry in St. Andrew's Register noted that he once served in Wolfe's army at Quebec, although his military service had ended sixty-seven years previously:

---

some experts believe that the sketch is not "consistent with Young's work," it is possible that it was only intended as a rough sketch and not as a final portrait. Based on Thompson-Harrower correspondence held at BAnQ, it is believed that a duplicate was made by Young and given to the Thompson family. In 1939 Thompson's grandson, James Thompson Harrower, arranged to have photographic copies made. One copy was given to BAnQ and has since gone missing. Another copy was acquired by LAC, part of the Milborne Masonic Collection, R3052-0-6E, accession number 1977-100. It is this photographic copy which is shown in this book.

290. *Ibid.*, Anecdote 8.
291. R. Byham to James Thompson, London, 24 December 1828, James T. Harrower Papers, CWM. In a side note to Anecdote 38, James Thompson Jr. wrote: "My father's Full Pay had been 7/6 per day – In consequence of this Appeal he was allowed a Retiring Allowance of 11/4 per day."
292. James Thompson to R. Byham, Quebec, 28 April 1829, James T. Harrower Papers, CWM.
293. JTC.

Mr. James Thompson, who belonged to a Highland Regiment which formed part of General Wolfe's Army at the taking of Quebec on the 13th day of September 1759, aged 97 years 5 months and 10 days here on the morning of the 25th instant & was buried on the 27th day of August 1830. James Harkness, Minister.[294]

Two days later, Thompson's remains were conveyed from St. Andrew's "to the Protestant cemetery on St. John Street" with full military (and presumably Masonic) honours, "attended by a large number of mourners."[295] The band and firing party were furnished by the 15th (The Yorkshire East Riding) Regiment, the garrison's senior British corps. As fate would have it, in 1759 the old 15th Foot (Amherst's Regiment) had been brigaded with Fraser's Highlanders on the Plains of Abraham.[296]

An interesting anecdote about the funeral was published in the Montreal *Gazette* on 26 January 1833. Sometime around 1760, William Moseley, then quartermaster sergeant of the 15th Regiment, had given Thompson a silver neck stock buckle[297] which Moseley had worn during the siege of Quebec, likely in exchange for a regimental memento from Thompson. In any event, this buckle was passed down to James Jr. When making funeral arrangements for his father, he had specifically requested that the quartermaster sergeant of the 15th Regiment be in command of the firing party. In appreciation for his services during

---

294. Register Book, St. Andrew's Church. The Rev. James Harkness was Minister between 1820 and 1835.
295. Gale, *Historic Tales*, 34. Another account, published in the *Quebec Chronicle* on 20 December 1918, stated that he was "buried with military honors in St. Matthew's Cemetery." Land for the Protestant cemetery on St. John Street had been purchased in 1771, with the first burial taking place in July 1772. When St. Matthew's Church was erected in 1822, the old cemetery became associated with the church (le cimetière Saint-Mathieu, rue Saint-Jean), although it was always known to the English as the St. John Street Cemetery. Some burials were affected when St. John Street was widened in 1845, and also when a piece in the southwest corner of the cemetery was sold to a private party (date unknown), and these may have impacted Thompson's family plot. When the cemetery closed in 1860 (it is now a park in Old Quebec), many families elected to have the remains of their loved ones relocated to other cemeteries, such as the newly opened Mount Herman in nearby Sillery. Designated as a historic monument in 1976, St. Matthew's Church was opened as a library in 1980 (Bibliothèque Saint-Jean-Baptiste). In spite of the fact that almost 7,000 burials took place, the current Register lists only 315 tombstones. Thompson's tombstone does not appear on this list. While it is possible that Thompson's remains were relocated to another cemetery, the editors believe that he rests in an unmarked grave in St. Matthew's Cemetery.
296. This regiment is known today as the Yorkshire Regiment. At Quebec in 1759, the 15th did not form up alongside the 78th on the main battle line, but provided left flank protection along with two battalions of the Royal Americans. The other regiment in garrison in Quebec in 1830 was the 66th Regiment (Berkshire).
297. In the 18th century, neck stocks were worn around the neck, over the shirt collar. The neck stock was adjusted at the back of the neck with a buckle or a pair of clasps.

the funeral, James Jr. presented Quartermaster Sergeant Biswick with the silver stock buckle that had been worn by his predecessor on the Plains of Abraham.

Thompson's obituary, published in the *Star and Commercial Advertiser* on 25 August 1830 reads in part:

> … Mr. Thompson possessed qualities of no ordinary kind. He was distinguished for an extraordinary degree of equanimity, which did not forsake him to the last, notwithstanding the severe illness with which he has for some months been afflicted. He was noted for his singularly correct and retentive memory with regard especially to the military transactions in which he had been engaged and from the recital of which his numerous friends have on numberless occasions derived peculiar pleasure. The strictest integrity, and regular attention to religious duties marked his conduct through life.

On 28 August the obituary editor added the following comment on the funeral procession as well as Thompson's character:

> Yesterday took place the funeral of the late Mr. James Thompson … in addition to the military honours due to his services, a very large concourse of civilians attended to pay their last respects to so distinguished a citizen. The bell of Saint Andrew's Church tolled its solemn knell, and the band of the 15th Regiment accompanied the procession with a march suitable to the mournful occasion … the pall was borne by military officers. The several grenadier companies in the garrison attended. The whole appearance was awfully solemn … one trait of his character, it would be unpardonable to omit. Unacquainted with fear, he never learned the art of using the slightest disguise of his sentiments, to suit the humour of any company. Naturally and truly humane, he was yet blunt, uniform, and undeviating in his statement of facts. Lord Dalhousie had the sagacity to see and appreciate the merits of this veteran and paid him much attention … we have already noticed his attention to religious duties. At the age of 96 he was to be seen assisting at the communion table.

The family erected a gravestone with the following inscription:

Sacred
to the Memory of
MR JAMES THOMPSON
(of Tain, in Scotland)
Overseer of Military Works
for the Garrison of Quebec
Who departed this Life
the 25th August 1830
Aged 98 Years[298]

---

298. Undated manuscript, James T. Harrower Papers, CWM. See also, BAnQ, P254-1972-00-085/7.

Shortly after his father's death, James Jr. began the painstaking task of transcribing his father's anecdotes, still on loose sheets of paper, into a two-volume set of letter-books "to give them a more ... secure form."[299]

Fanny Thompson died two years after her beloved husband, succumbing to cholera on 19 July 1832.[300] Upon her death, the family residence on St. Ursula Street, as well as her husband's material possessions (his journals, diaries, broadsword, dirks, as well as General Richard Montgomery's sword) were passed on to the eldest son, James Jr., in accordance with her husband's wishes. Over the winter of 1832–33, the Thompson house on St. Ursula Street remained vacant. About this same time, it was divided into two distinct residences and it became a rental property until 1839, when it was again occupied by descendants of James Thompson.

Following the death of James Jr. in 1869, everything reverted to his nephew, James Thompson Harrower, and his niece, Annie Harrower. Some years later, the Harrowers became interested in selling General Montgomery's sword, which had been valued at $500.[301] Until a buyer could be found, however, they allowed it to be exhibited in the Literary and Historical Society of Quebec. In 1878, the Marquess of Lorne, then Governor General of Canada, purchased it for the "exceeding low price of $150.00."[302] The Harrowers had accepted this low purchase amount only because they believed that the representative of the British Crown "would be a worthy owner of such a famous relic."[303] However, to their great indignation, the Marquess turned around and handed the sword back to representatives of the Livingstone family of New York, Montgomery's nearest American relations, who in turn eventually entrusted it to the Smithsonian Institution.[304]

---

299. JTC – Introduction by James Thompson Jr. This set, and a second single-volume version more suitable for public consumption, are covered in detail in our editors' Preface.
300. Fanny was seventy-three years of age and in good health until she was afflicted. Her grave cannot be located, but family records state that she was buried next to her husband (BAnQ, P254-1972-00-085).
301. On 6 October 1895, the *New York Times* published an article on the sale of General Montgomery's sword indicating that James Thompson Harrower had originally wanted $1,000 for it.
302. Frederick Christian Wurtele, "Note on Montgomery's Sword," LHSQ, *Historical Documents*, Series 7 (1905); C. Stuart to J.T. Harrower, the Citadel, Quebec, undated, James Thompson Harrower Papers, CWM. Stuart was secretary to the Marquess of Lorne.
303. *Ibid*.
304. *Ibid*. The sword, known as a hanger, was presented to Congress by Miss Julia Burton Hunt in 1923 and subsequently deposited in the Smithsonian Institution in Washington, D.C.

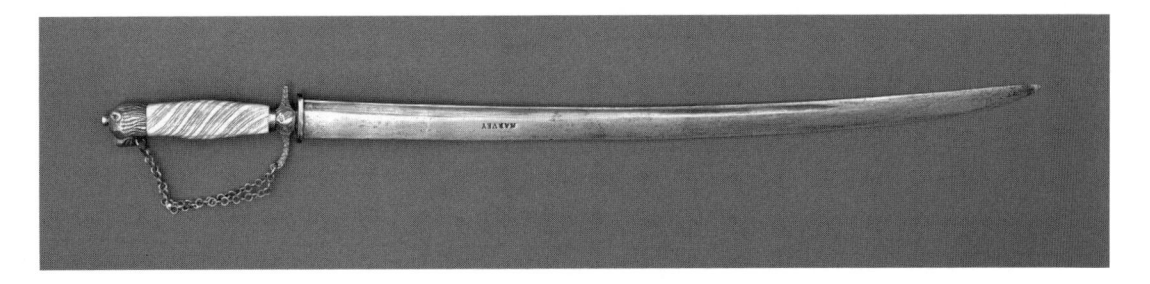

"A poor looking thing." James Thompson acquired General Richard Montgomery's personal sword after his death on New Year's Eve during the siege of Quebec 1776-77. He described it thus: "It has a head at the top of the hilt, somewhat resembling a lion's or bull dog's, with crop'd ears, the edges indented, with a ring passing through the chin or under-jaw, from which is suspended a double silver chain communicating with the front tip of the guard, by a second ring; at the lower end of the handle there is, on each side, the figure of a spread eagle.... The handle itself is of ivory, and undulated obliquely from top to bottom. The blade which is twenty-two inches long, and fluted near the back, is single-edged, with a slight curve towards the point...." He would also claim (Anecdote 17) that it was "altogether but a poor looking thing," but a magnet for "receiving the visits of a great number of American Ladies and Gentlemen...." (Smithsonian Institution, Washington D.C., 72-1151)

The Thompson house on St. Ursula Street remained in the family until 3 June 1957, when, despite Thompson's wish that it always remain in his family, it was sold to Mr. Pietre Farago for $7,000 with part of the land sold to Dr. Jacques Boulanger (by this time, the Thompson male lineage had died out). In April 1958 Mr. Willy Côté bought the house and sold it three years later to the Ministry of Cultural Affairs of the Province of Quebec (Ministère des Affaires culturelles du Québec) for $18,500. On 21 February 1961, after having being renamed "Maison Côté," the old Thompson house was declared a historic monument in Quebec (notwithstanding the fact that Côté's only role was to make a quick profit).

Over the period 1964–70 the house was restored under the direction of architect André Robitaille and used as an office by the Ministry of Cultural Affairs. In 1965 research undertaken by historian Michel Gaumond showed that the old house should not be known as "Maison Côté" but rather as "Maison Thompson." In true bureaucratic fashion, the name was changed to "Maison Thompson-Côté."[305]

The commemorative plaque attached to the building translates as follows:

---

305. Private correspondence with Christian Rioux, July 2009.

QUÉBEC

MAISON JAMES THOMPSON

This house was built in 1793
by James Thompson, supervisor of
military works for his Majesty, George III,
on land yielded in 1789 by the
Ursulines to Charles Cornélier dit
Grandchamp. His descendants
lived here until 1957.

James Thompson, born at Tain, Ross-shire
Scotland, in 1732, died at Quebec, 25 August 1830, at
ninety-eight years of age.

MINISTÈRE DES AFFAIRES CULTURELLES
COMMISSION DES MONUMENTS HISTORIQUES[306]

In 1995, needing funds to restore other houses in Quebec, perhaps those with a more distinct "French" heritage, the government sold the old Thompson house to Mr. Greg Alexander, a retired fireman from Toronto, on the strict condition that it be restored as close as possible to its original construction (the house still maintained its designation as a Quebec historic monument). Today, Maison Historique James Thompson is a popular bed and breakfast in the historic part of Quebec City, the oldest surviving house in Quebec with an "English chimney arrangement" on the gable points. Its extra pair of chimneys are set equidistantly along the roof-ridge, "another English feature."[307]

There can be no doubt that James Thompson, and the other soldiers of the 78th Fraser Highlanders who settled in Quebec after the regiment was disbanded in Glasgow in December 1763,[308] had a profound impact on the development of Canada. The descendants of these Highlanders may still be found in the towns, villages and farms along the banks of the St. Lawrence River, and some have spread across Canada and the United States. Of those who remained in Quebec, many married into French-Canadian families and are now completely francophone, "and from whom all other traces of their Scottish ancestry, save the occa-

---

306. The Historic Monuments Commission of the Ministry of Cultural Affairs for the Province of Quebec must have had second thoughts about calling the house Maison Thompson-Côté, as the name on the plaque simply reads "Maison James Thompson."
307. A.J.H. Richardson, "Guide to the Architecturally and Historically Most Significant Buildings in the Old City of Quebec with a Biographical Dictionary of Architects and Builders and Illustrations," *Bulletin of the Association for Preservation Technology*, vol 2, Nos. 3-4 (1970), 33.
308. *Gazetteer & London Daily Advertiser*, London, 26 December 1763, British Library, 17th–18th Century Burney Collection: "The 14th inst. Frazer's [sic] Highland regiment was broke at Glasgow: most of them had learned French during their residence at Quebec."

"Maison James Thompson." On 21 February 1961 Thompson's old house on the corner of St. Ursula Street and Ursulines Lane was declared a historic monument by the Historic Monuments Commission of the Ministry of Cultural Affairs. A French-only commemorative plaque was attached to the side of the building facing St. Ursula Street. (Photo by Earl John Chapman)

sional shock of red hair, have completely disappeared."[309] Notwithstanding this claim, a good percentage still maintain some aspects of their Scottish heritage, evidence of which is their enthusiastic support for Scottish societies in Quebec and the rest of Canada. They bring to these organizations a unique blend of the cultures which built Canada.

Colonel JAMES PATTISON COCKBURN, commanding the Royal Artillery at Quebec and a noted military artist, knew Thompson well. In 1831 he wrote an interesting summation of Thompson's life in his travel book:

> He was born in Tain, in Scotland, and came to this country in General Wolfe's army, and was at the capture of Louisbourg, and in the sanguinary but unsuccessful affair at Beauport. His memory enabled him at all times to relate many of the adventures of the different engagements which preceded the fall of Quebec. He also took part in the defense of this city against the attacks of the American Generals, Arnold and Montgomery, in December 1775. As a soldier he was intrepid; as a servant of the King he was strictly faithful. To these qualities he added many of the domestic virtues. He reared a numerous family, and his sons are now in situations of trust and honor.[310]

---

309. A.J.B. Milborne, "The Lodge in the 78th Regiment (Fraser's Highlanders)," *Quatuor Coronati Lodge*, vol LXV (1952) 19–33.
310. James Pattison Cockburn, *Quebec and its Environs: Being a Picturesque Guide to a Stranger* (Quebec, 1831), 38. Cockburn served as the commander of the Royal Artillery in the Canadas between 1826 and 1832, and so he would have known Thompson towards the end of his life. As a military artist, Cockburn's work is of inestimable documentary value for Canadian history. He was particularly interested in Quebec City, its architecture, narrow streets and picturesque landscapes.

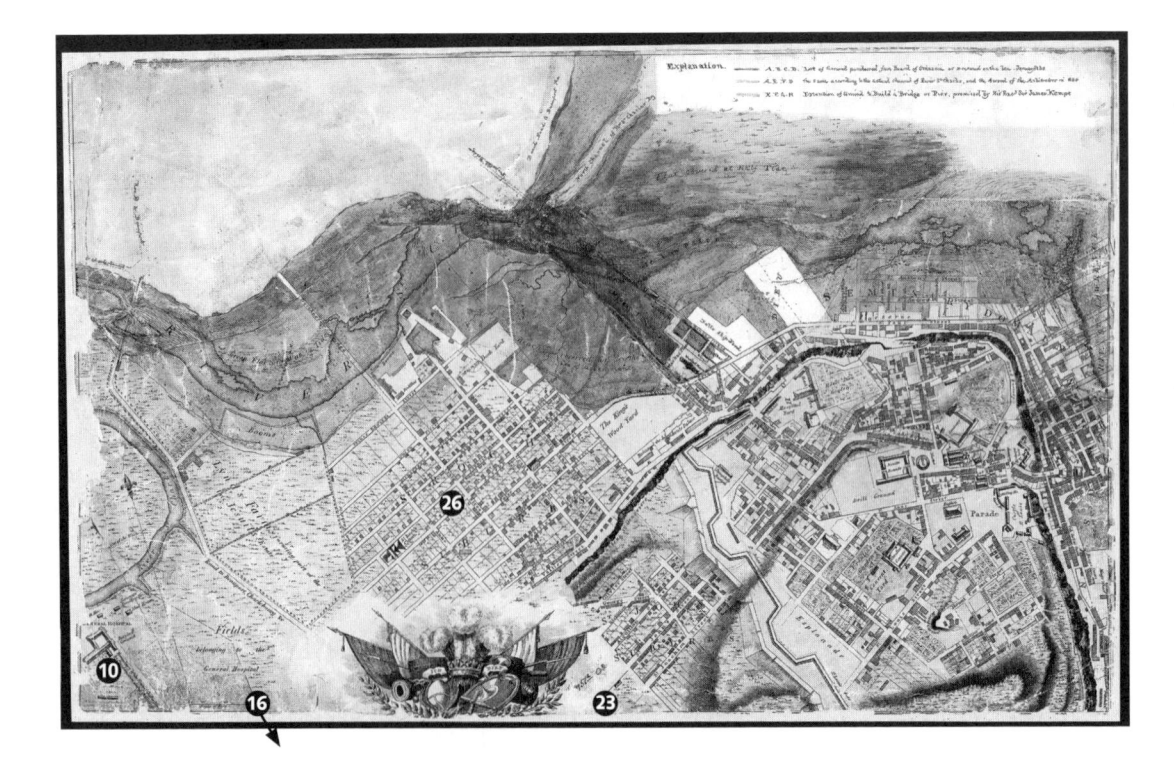

James Thompson's Quebec, 1830. The detail on the facing page, taken from Joseph Bouchette's "Plan of Quebec, 1830," shows the fortified city of Quebec at the time of Thompson's death. The entire map is shown above. (LAC NMC 1648.0)

1. Anglican Cathedral
2. Angel Street
3. Artillery Park
4. Bishop's Palace
5. Château St. Louis and Château Haldimand
6. Citadel
7. Esplanade
8. Free Masons' Hall (Buade Street)
9. Hope Gate
10. Hôpital général (General Hospital)
11. Hôtel-Dieu
12. Intendant's Palace
13. Jesuits Barracks (Jesuits College)
14. Palace Gate
15. Palace Street (rue des Pauvres)
16. Plains of Abraham
17. Royal Engineers Yard and Complex
18. Seminary
19. St. Andrew's Presbyterian Church
20. St. Anne Street
21. St. John Gate
22. St. John Street
23. St. John Street Protestant Cemetery
24. St. Louis Gate
25. St. Louis Street
26. St. Roch suburb
27. Thompson's House (St. Ursula Street)
28. Ursuline Convent
29. Wolfe's Corner (Wolfe's statue)
30. Wolfe–Montcalm monument

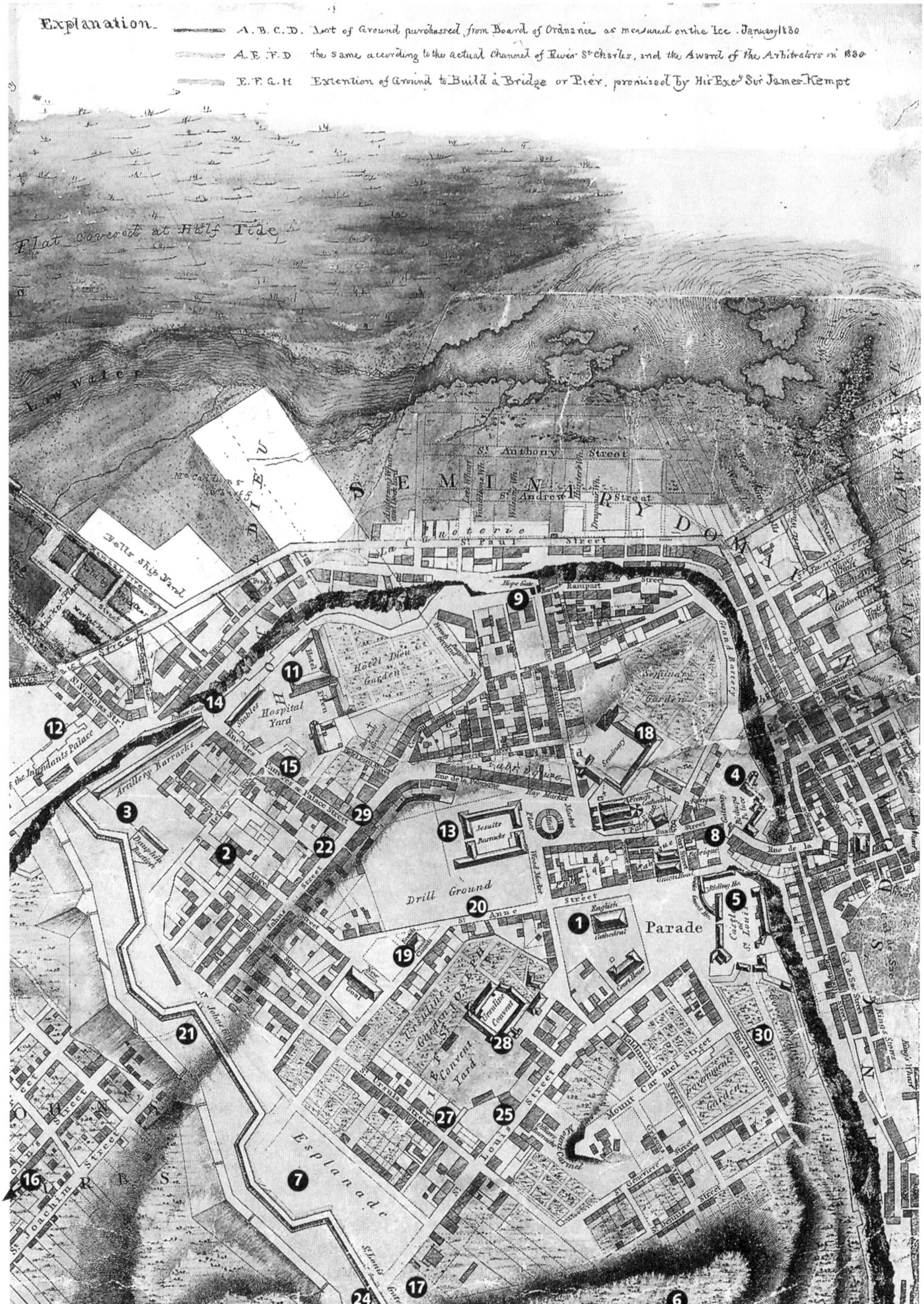
Explanation
A. B. C. D. Lot of Ground purchassed from Board of Ordnance as measured on the Ice. January 1830
A. E. F. D the same according to the actual Channel of River St Charles, and the Award of the Arbitrators in 1830
E. F. G. H Extention of Ground to Build a Bridge or Pier, promised by His Exc'y Sir James Kempt
Flat covered at Half Tide
Low Water
St. Anthony Street
St. Andrew Street
SEMINARY DOMAIN
St. Paul Street
Bells Ship Yard
Rampart
Grand Battery
Hotel Dieu Garden
Hospital Yard
Stables
St. Nicholas Str.
the Intendants Palace
Artillery Barracks
Dauphin Barracks
Palace Street
Jesuits Barracks
Hay Market
Seminary Garden
Seminary
French Cathedral
Drill Ground
St. Anne Street
English Cathedral
Parade
Riding Ho.
Castle of St. Louis
Court House
Ursuline Garden
Ursuline Convent
Convent Yard
Esplanade
St. Ursule Street
St. Louis Street
Mount Carmel Street
Mount Carmel
Government Garden
St. Louis Gate
St. Johns Street
St. Joachim Street
Kings Street
Kings Wharf
1
2
3
4
5
6
7
8
9
11
12
13
14
15
16
17
18
19
20
21
22
24
25
27
28
29
30

"Here died Wolfe, victorious." These were the words originally inscribed on General Wolfe's monument on the Plains of Abraham. In 1832 a truncated granite pillar was erected by Governor General Lord Matthew Whitmore-Aylmer, the first "real" monument to the fallen hero, replacing a boulder that marked the place Wolfe died. By 1849 it had deteriorated and was replaced by a Doric column topped by a bronze helmet and sword. The 1832 plaque was retained and a new one added to show that the new monument was a gift of the British army in Canada, under the command of Lieutenant General Sir Benjamin D'Urban. After more than a half century of weathering, this monument was replaced in 1913 by the National Battlefields Commission, keeping the same plaques and head pieces but adding a third plaque describing the history of the preceding monuments. On 29 March 1963, the monument was destroyed by French-Canadian nationalists who believed that it stood as "an affront to their dignity." It was re-erected in July 1965 with new bilingual plaques. However, the word "victorious" was omitted. While the removal of the offending word did not appease French-Canadian sensibilities, it raised controversy in the Anglophone community. Standing in front of the Musée national des beaux-arts du Québec, Wolfe's monument continues to be a focal point for Quebec nationalists. (Photo by Earl John Chapman)

"The bell of Saint Andrew's Church tolled its solemn knell…." So wrote the obituary writer of the *Star and Commercial Advertiser* on 28 August 1830 when covering the funeral of James Thompson, adding that the "band of the 15th regiment accompanied the procession with a march suitable to the mournful occasion." Thompson had been laid to rest the previous day, his pall "borne by military officers." One of the oldest Protestant burial grounds preserved in Quebec, the "old cemetery on St. John street" has been transformed into a public garden – a haven of peace in a densely-populated urban centre. Land for the cemetery had been purchased from the nuns of the Hôtel-Dieu in 1771, with the first burial taking place the following summer. When St. Matthew's Church was erected in 1822, the old cemetery became associated with the church (le cimetière Saint-Mathieu, rue Saint-Jean), although it was always known to the English as the St. John Street Cemetery. In spite of the fact that almost 7,000 burials took place up to the cemetery's closing in 1860, the register book lists only 315 tombstones. While Thompson's tombstone does not appear on this list, the editors believe that he still rests here in an unmarked grave, alongside his beloved Fanny. (Photo by Earl John Chapman)

A COLOUR ALBUM

1. **"Election of the Grand Master."** In this mural by Charles W. Kelsey (1877–1975), one of six adorning the Memorial Hall of Montreal's Masonic Memorial Temple, Quebec's military Masons, drawn from all the regiments of Wolfe's army, assembled on 28 November 1759 in one of the few buildings left standing after the bombardment of the city. Their mission was to establish the first Grand Lodge in Canada and to install Lieutenant John Price Guinnett (47th Foot) as their first Provincial Grand Master. The artist included some other notable Masons, among them Lieutenant Colonel Simon Fraser (78th Foot); Provost Marshal Miles Prentice (43rd Foot); Sergeant Alexander "Sandy" Simpson (78th Foot); and Sergeant James Thompson (the tall Mason standing behind the dais in the centre of the mural). The artist took pains to delineate Thompson's features accurately, basing them on a portrait (see frontispiece) by Captain John Crawford Young of the 79th Regiment in August 1828. (Courtesy: Éditions Point de Fuite, Montreal)

2. **"Three Mystic Taps."** In this mural by Charles W. Kelsey (1877–1975), another of the six at Montreal's Masonic Memorial Temple, James Thompson is shown giving the "mystic three strokes with the Mallet" on the cornerstone of the Wolfe–Montcalm Monument in Quebec, under the watchful eye of the Right Worshipful Brother Claude Dénéchau, Provincial Grand Master, standing across the stone from Thompson. Thompson, in his ninety-fifth year, needed the physical support of Captain John Crawford Young of the 79th Highlanders. The Earl of Dalhousie is shown on the far right, and Thompson's son, William Alexander Thompson, can be seen standing to the right of Claude Dénéchau. (Courtesy: Éditions Point de Fuite, Montreal)

3. **Lieutenant Colonel Simon Fraser, 1759.** This detail from a digital copy of the painting *The Death of General James Wolfe* completed by Benjamin West in 1770 shows Colonel Simon Fraser of the 78th Foot (the man with the ginger hair) wearing a full belted plaid. In West's painting, the plaid appears to be a brownish red sett with broad green, double red and black stripes. In fact, Fraser was neither at the battle nor present at Wolfe's death. This detail is believed to be the only extant image of Simon Fraser. Other images previously identified as the *"Mac Shimi"* have been now identified as his nephew and heir, Archibald Campbell Fraser, who was a colonel commanding the Fraser Fencibles during the Napoleonic Wars. (Image detail, Editor's Collection)

4. **James Thompson Jr.** This pen and ink sketch shows James Jr. in 1846, then a newly-minted deputy commissary general and a resident of St. Johns, Quebec. He is shown with his dog and double-barrelled firearm, no doubt a nod to his prowess as a hunter. A note on the back reads, "Present from Mrs. Lister on her leaving St. Johns and, 13th June 1846, to D.C.G. Thompson." It was James Jr. who ensured the survival of his father's oral histories and memories by recording and organizing them. (CWM 2008026-001)

5. **"Wolfe's Corner, Quebec, 1830."** From the junction of Palace and St. John streets, we look westward towards the inner face of the St. John Gate. On the right stands Joseph Vaillancourt's tavern and grocery store with an inviting sign above the door displaying a keg and drying herbs. In the corner niche above the ground floor stands Wolfe's statue, executed by the sculptor brothers Thomas-Hyacinthe and Ives Chaulette, with

the assistance of James Thompson (see Anecdote 8). This property was purchased in April 1780 by butcher George Hipps, a former soldier in Wolfe's army, who decided to use the empty niche "to some higher purpose." Hipps could not think of anyone more worthy of the honour than the famous general under whom he had served. Watercolour by James Pattison Cockburn. (Royal Ontario Museum 951x205.17)

6. Château St. Louis, 1829. Standing between the Château Haldimand (right) and the Château St. Louis (left), we look towards the Citadel buildings located straight ahead on the Cape Diamond promontory. Construction of the simpler Château Haldimand was begun in 1784 by Governor Frederick Haldimand and the building was inaugurated three years later by his successor, Lord Dorchester. The elegantly-attired officers of the 15th Foot seen here, resplendent with shining swords and fancy headgear, are typical of the privileged persons who frequented the hallowed precincts of the governor's quarters. The corporal's headgear is the bell-top shako and he is using his left hand to salute (up to 1867 either arm was used for saluting, depending upon which side an officer was approaching). In January 1834, shortly after the artist recorded this scene, the splendid Château St. Louis was destroyed by fire while Governor-in-Chief Lord Aylmer was in residence. In 1838 Lord Durham had the ruins taken away to allow the construction of a panoramic terrace. Watercolour by James Pattison Cockburn. (Royal Ontario Museum 942.48.87)

7. Justice Jonathan Sewell's house and the St. Louis Gate, 1829. From the corner of St. Louis and D'Auteuil streets, we look toward the interior side of the St. Louis Gate. The elegant house behind the row of trees was built 1803–04 for the powerful Chief Justice Sewell, who still resided there when the artist made this drawing. The squat building with hipped roof and two chimneys to the right of the Sewell house is the Royal Engineers Office, where Thompson worked in his later years, and which now forms part of the fashionable Garrison Club. The engineers relocated here to be close to the Citadel during its final construction in the 1820s and early '30s. The military parade ground, known as the Esplanade, appears on the right, separated from the streets by a low wood fence. Watercolour by James Pattison Cockburn. (Royal Ontario Museum 942.48.85)

8. Snuff mull. James Thompson's small ram's-horn snuff mull (see Anecdote 32) was given to him by his friend Captain Charles Grant in 1776. The lid was originally "mounted" by a London silversmith; Thompson had it replaced in 1821 by James Smillie, a Quebec silversmith. At the same time he had a "Scotch pebble" set into the lid. When the mull was passed down to his son, the words "James Thompson, 1733, to his son James, 1784" were engraved across the edge. Acquired by Montreal's McCord Museum in March 1972 along with three pages (Anecdotes 30 and 31) that had been cut out of the manuscript letter-book now in the possession of the Stewart Museum. (McCord Museum M972.46.2)

9. Silver thistle cup. James Thompson's small silver cup (see Anecdote 30) was made by Tain silversmith Hugh Ross, likely about 1710. It is made of heavy-gauge silver and the words "I MK – Tain, Ross-shire, 1637" are engraved above the girdle. Acquired by the McCord Museum in March 1972 with the snuff mull and letter-book pages noted above. (McCord Museum M972.46.1)

10. "Murder dirk." James Thompson's first dirk (the shorter of the two in the colour photograph) was made from an old sword blade while the 78th Foot was quartered in Stratford, Connecticut, over the winter of 1757–58. This is the dirk with which Sergeant Alexander Fraser killed Corporal James Macky in a fight in Stratford's guardhouse (see Anecdote 12). Thompson carved the wooden handle with a Masonic emblem and a local silversmith secured it to the blade.

The symbolism of freemasonry is based on the geometrical tools of the medieval mason, such as the dividers and square, as seen in the handle detail at right. The letter "G" is the Masonic symbol representing God, the Deity, and Geometry.

On the other side of this dirk, Thompson carved two interlocked hearts likely symbolizing brotherly love, an important concept reflecting the connection of all Masons in common brotherhood.

Smaller dirks like these are thought to have been worn concealed under the arm. The longer of the two was made sometime later and is carved with an elaborate Celtic knot-work design, presumably by Thompson. The silver mount of the larger dirk is engraved with his name "Ja: Thompson" in a script closely resembling his personal signature. Both dirks were passed down through the Thompson family and later acquired by the Canadian War Museum. (CWM 19720103-007/8)

11. Montgomery's sword. This sword, known as a hanger, which belonged to American commander Brigadier Richard Montgomery, was picked up by a British drummer boy following the general's death leading the failed night assault on Quebec, 31 December 1775 (see Anecdote 29). Thompson gave the boy seven shillings and six pence, and the sword was passed down through the Thompson family until it was purchased by Governor General the Marquis of Lorne in 1878. It was subsequently passed to the *chargé d'affaires* of the British Legation in Washington in 1881 and was presented to Montgomery's descendant Louise Livingston Hunt. The latter's sister, Judy Barton Hunt, eventually presented it to the United States Congress, which deposited it in the Smithsonian Institution, where it resides today. (Smithsonian Institution, Washington D.C., 72-1151)

12. Nuns knitting at General Hospital. A late 19th-century depiction of five Highlanders of the 78th Foot (incorrectly identified as the Highland Guards) convalescing at Quebec's Hôpital général, presumably after having been wounded at either the battle on the Plains of Abraham in 1759 or at Sillery in 1760. Two nuns are shown seated at the right, knitting long grey socks for the soldiers, an activity mentioned by Lieutenant John Knox in his *Journals*. Watercolour by John H. Macnaughton, active 1876–99. (LAC R1818-0-2-E)

13. A private soldier of the 78th Foot, 1759. The dress and weapons of a Highland regiment were, without a doubt, the most distinguishing features that set them apart from a standard Georgian marching regiment of the day. The promise of going to war in the "garb of their fathers" and wielding Highland weapons cannot be understated, for even the bards mention this great honour being accorded to the young soldiers going off to fight in the Seven Years' War. In this modern reconstruction by Douglas N. Anderson, a private soldier of the 78th Foot (Fraser's Highlanders) wears (from the top down) a dark blue bonnet with black ribbon cockade above the left eye, acting as an anchor for a strip of black bearskin; a white linen shirt under a short scarlet jacket with off-white facings; belted plaid consisting of up to 12 yards of tartan tweed five feet wide; black leather waist belt with cartridge box; a sporran; red-and-white diced hose held up with red garters; and black leather shoes fastened with brass buckles. The Highlander is shown fully armed with a .75-calibre smooth-bore Short Land musket (a carbine originally intended for use by mounted troops), a plain but sturdy "Jeffreys" basket-hilted backsword, a dirk, an all-metal Highland-pattern pistol and a socket-type bayonet. (Stewart Museum, Montreal)

14. The modern Frasers. The pipes and drums of the modern-day 78th Fraser Highlanders march through the gate of Fort Île-Ste-Hélène, a historic site on Montreal's St. Helen's Island. Constructed by the British army in the early 1820s, it served an important purpose as the central artillery depot for all forts west, including Fort Henry and Fort Lennox. Falling into disrepair, Fort Île-Ste-Hélène was restored in the 1930s as a public works initiative during the Great Depression. Today the fort is the home of the Stewart Museum, an institution founded in 1955 to collect, store and display historical artifacts from Canada's colonial past, particularly that of New France. In the mid-1960s, the museum launched its military demonstration program when two 18th century regiments were raised: Les Compagnies franches de la Marine and the Olde 78th Fraser Highlanders. During summer months, the two reconstituted regiments perform daily musket drills, as well as fife and drum and bagpipe performances that are a delight to tourists and local residents alike. (Stewart Museum, Montreal)

1. "Election of the Grand Master."

2. "Three Mystic Taps."

3. Lieutenant Colonel Simon Fraser, 1759.

4. James Thompson Jr.

5. "Wolfe's Corner, Quebec, 1830."

6. Château St. Louis, 1829 (below).

7. Justice Jonathan Sewell's house and the St. Louis Gate, 1829.

8. Snuff mull.

9. Silver cup.

10. "Murder dirk."

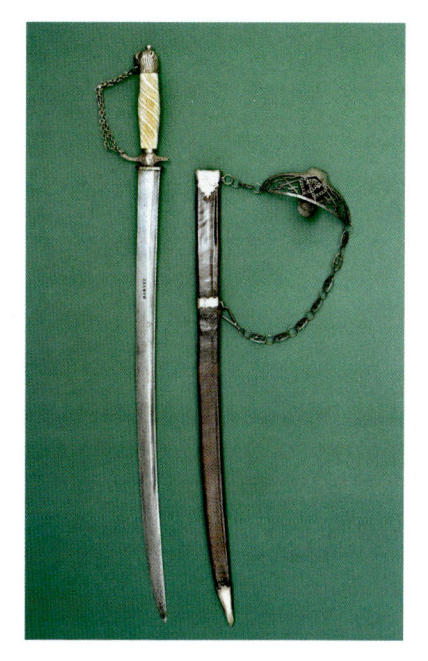

11. Montgomery's sword (right).

12. Nuns knitting at General Hospital.

13. The Highland soldier.

14. The modern Frasers.